THE MODERN NATIONS IN
HISTORICAL PERSPECTIVE

ROBIN W. WINKS, *General Editor*

The volumes in this series deal with individual nations or
groups of closely related nations, summarizing the chief historical trends
and influences that have contributed to each nation's present-day character, problems, and behavior. Recent data are incorporated with established
historical background to achieve a fresh synthesis and original interpretation.

The author of this volume, KENNETH SCOTT LATOURETTE, has written
definitively on China and the Far East. He is the author of *The Chinese:
Their History and Culture* and *A Short History of the Far East*, among
numerous other works. He is Sterling Professor of Missions and Oriental
History and Fellow of Berkeley College (Emeritus) at Yale University.

FORTHCOMING VOLUMES IN THE ASIAN SUBSERIES

Buddhist Lands of Southeast Asia *by John F. Cady*
Ceylon *by S. Arasaratnam*
India *by Stanley Wolpert*
Indonesia *by J. D. Legge*
Japan *by John W. Hall*
Malaysia *by John Bastin*
Pakistan *by A. R. Mallick*
The Philippines *by Onofre D. Corpuz*

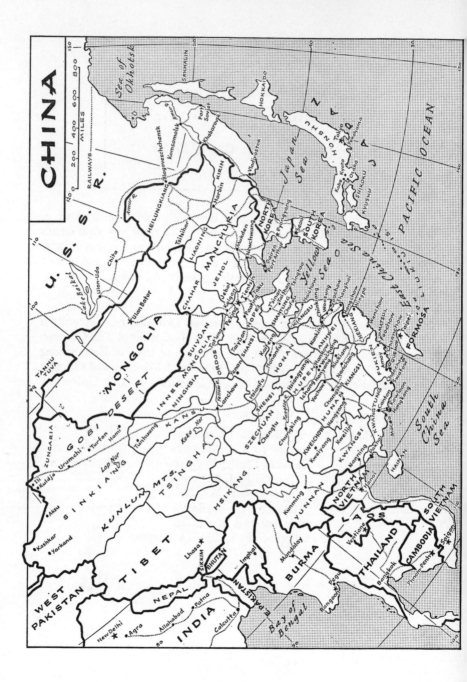

C H I N A

KENNETH SCOTT LATOURETTE

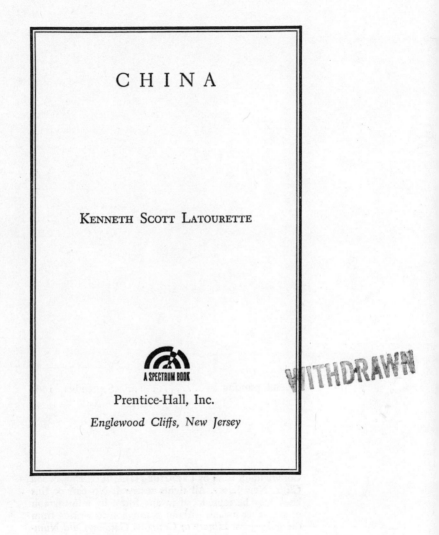

A SPECTRUM BOOK

Prentice-Hall, Inc.

Englewood Cliffs, New Jersey

Second printing .... September, 1965

Copyright © 1964 by PRENTICE-HALL, INC., *Englewood Cliffs, New Jersey.* All rights reserved. No part of this book may be reproduced in any form, by mimeograph or any other means, without permission in writing from the publishers. *Library of Congress Catalog Card Number:* 64-23560. Printed in the United States of America —C. P 13256, C 13266

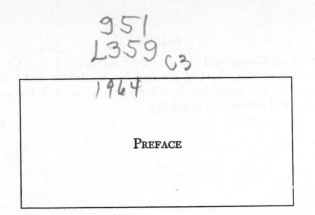

PREFACE

China is a subject of major importance to all the world. The Chinese mainland encompasses the largest fairly homogeneous portion of mankind. China has long had a unique and highly developed civilization, which profoundly influenced its neighbors—Japan, Korea, and what we now call North Vietnam.

Since the mid-nineteenth century China has been caught up in a revolution that has affected all phases of life. The China of the 1950's and 1960's is experiencing a major stage of that revolution. No other great people today is being so drastically and so rapidly transformed. The changes now taking place have been shaped by what has come out of both the remote and the recent past. Thus, an understanding of China's modern revolution and of the cataclysmic changes of the 1950's and 1960's must be based on a knowledge of Chinese history.

Four questions are of general concern: (1) Why did the Communists succeed in taking over the mainland? (2) How successfully have they carried out their aims between 1949 and the present? (3) How much of the old China persists? and (4) What now are the prospects for continued control of the mainland by the Communists? This book seeks answers to the first three questions. The fourth entails prophecy, which the historian must not venture; he can merely point out possible or likely alternatives.

No historian, however, writes without a bias. If he claims to be objective, he is either self-deceived or dishonest. I confess to two seemingly contradictory biases. On the one hand, I have a great admiration for the Chinese and a deep affection for my many Chinese friends. On the other hand, I view the Communist domination of the mainland as a major tragedy, both for the Chinese and for all mankind. That domination arose from circumstances for which the Chinese as a whole were not responsible,

v

yet which made Communist victory almost inevitable. I view Communist rule as only a passing phase of the ongoing revolution that will be the chief theme of this book, but how long that phase will last and what will follow I will not venture to predict.

K.S.L.

CONTENTS

vii

ONE

THE CONTEMPORARY SCENE

In the 1950's and early 1960's China has been divided and governed by two governments. Each claims to be the legitimate one for all China; both regard themselves as engaged in a civil war for control of the country, a civil war which had its beginnings in the 1920's. In the early 1950's the government in control of mainland China, which was now called the People's Republic of China (*Chung Hua Jên Min Kung Ho Kuo*), was dominated by the Chinese Communist Party. That party based its policies and ideals on the teachings of Karl Marx and esteemed V. I. Lenin as an authoritative commentator on Marx. Its organization was patterned on the party which controlled Russia, but the Chinese Communists insisted that their outstanding leader, Mao Tse-tung, was giving the correct interpretation to Marx.

The other government, from 1949, controlled the island of Formosa or Taiwan, now called the Republic of China (*Chung Hua Min Kuo*). As in the People's Republic of China this government too declared that it was a democracy. It, too, was dominated by one party, the Kuomintang ("the National People's Party"), usually known as the Nationalist Party. The Nationalists professed to follow the program of Sun Yat-sen, but since the 1920's their outstanding leader has been Chiang Kai-shek. In its structure, like the Chinese Communist Party, it has been influenced by the Communist Party of Russia, but in its ideals it has borne more of the impress of democ-

1

racy as the Anglo-Saxon West understands that term, and in it have been some who have sought to make that kind of democracy effective.

The history of the Chinese Communist Party before 1949 was checkered. The party was organized in 1920, and its initial national congress was convened in Shanghai in 1921. It was closely associated with the Communist International and was modeled on the Russian Communist Party. At the outset its dominant figure was Ch'ên Tu-hsiu (1878-1943), a man of scholar-official stock who had been trained in the Chinese classics. At twenty he rebelled against that tradition, journeyed to Japan where it was easily possible to imbibe the new currents from the West, returned to China in 1910, and became a leader of the youth who were seeking to remake their country. In the 1920's he became Dean of the College of Letters in Peking University (also known as Pei Ta), then a leading influence in the social and intellectual Renaissance, and he made it a nursery of revolutionists. By 1920 he had abandoned the Western idea of democracy and had become a convinced Marxist.

To achieve its ends, the Chinese Communist Party sought to infiltrate the *Kuomintang*, and in the 1920's, when the armies of the Kuomintang led by Chiang Kai-shek began a triumphal march northward from Canton, the Communists were present in their advance and in their wake. In 1927 a breach occurred between the Communists and Chiang Kai-shek and thenceforward Chiang attempted to eliminate them. The Communists divided into two rival factions: Ch'ên Tu-hsiu broke with those who cooperated with the Comintern; and he, a Trotskyite, was expelled from the party which he had founded. His prestige rapidly declined.

After these developments, Russian influence, previously strong but not unchallenged, waned and new Chinese leadership in the person of Mao Tse-tung took command. A native of the province of Hunan, from which some of the outstanding nineteenth-century leaders of the Empire had sprung, Mao Tse-tung (1893-   ) was of prosperous peasant stock. He early rebelled against his father's control, studied enough of the older literature to acquire familiarity with it, went to Changsha, the capital of Hunan, and in 1918 graduated from the provincial normal school. There he was caught up in the revolutionary movement and was thrilled by the writings of Ch'ên Tu-hsiu. To prepare himself for leadership he became an ardent physical culturist and laid the foundations for his remarkable athletic vigor. Later, he enrolled at Peking University, and by the summer of 1920 he had become a convinced Marxist; in 1921 he became affiliated with the Chinese Communist Party. Disagreeing with the orthodox Communist theory that the socialist revolution must spring from the industrial proletariat, he held that it must arise among the peasants. For a time he was not in the good graces of the party, but in 1931 he was again accepted and ultimately became its leader.

Chou En-lai (1898-   ), another of the quartet of Communist leaders after 1949, came from a scholarly background: his father had been an official under the Empire. While a student in France after World War I, Chou En-lai became a Communist, and after his return to China, he was soon prominent in Communist councils. In manners he represents the traditional Chinese intellectual gentleman, able to be charming and suave when he chooses. Not a creative thinker, he has been known as an able administrator and a shrewd diplomat.

Liu Shao-ch'i (c. 1898 or 1905-   ), third in the quartet, was, like Mao, from Hunan and of peasant stock. He too graduated from the provincial normal school in Changsha. He was early a Socialist, was repeatedly in Russia, and has come to be regarded by foreigners as the theoretician of the Chinese Communist Party. In his first days as a revolutionist, in contrast with Mao who centered his activities on the peasants, he cultivated the miners and the labor unions. Dour, severe, he does not have the *bonhomie* of Mao or the charm of Chou. However, in later years he became a spokesman for Mao Tse-tung.

Chu Tê (1886-   ), the military member of the quartet, in his boyhood in the province of Szechwan, was given a traditional classical training. But he was an activist who had become aware of the new currents from the West. After graduation from a military institution, for a time he was on the road to becoming one of the warlords who ruled China in the stormy early years of the Republic; then for a time he was an adherent of Sun Yat-sen. However, while he was a student in Germany in the 1920's he was converted to communism, and, returning to China, he joined Mao and became the commander-in-chief of the Communist army.

Not a member of the quartet, but in the 1960's with mounting influence was Ch'en Yi. Younger than the others, he had studied in France, as head of the guerrillas had been left in the Southeast when the others departed on the Long March, in 1949 captured Shanghai, and by 1963 was Vice Premier and Foreign Minister.

After the break with Chiang Kai-shek in the 1920's, the Communists sought to carry out their program in rural sections southeast of the Yangtze River. There they were pressed so hard by Chiang's armies that in 1934-1935 on what became known as the "Long March," the leaders and their followers made their way by difficult and perilous mountain routes to the northwest, and established their capital at Yenan. Chiang Kai-shek still attempted to eliminate them. He went north in December, 1936, to urge his subordinate, Chang Hsüeh-liang, to press the campaign more vigorously. Chang believed that the Kuomintang and the Communists should join forces against the Japanese, who were then progressively bringing the north under their control, and he therefore seized Chiang, who, to obtain his liberty, entered into an ostensible peace with the Communists: the two professed to present a common front against the acute threat of the Japanese advance. Thenceforward Chang Hsüeh-liang was under Kuomintang surveillance and spent his later days in Taiwan.

From its headquarters in Yenan, under Mao Tse-tung's leadership, the Chinese Communist Party consolidated its structure and created an army, chiefly of peasants disciplined in Communist ideals. The Communists carried on successful guerrilla resistance to the Japanese, but they did not, as did Chiang's troops, bear the main brunt of the Japanese invasion. Stalin looked upon them coolly, for their program of basing the revolution upon the peasants rather than the industrial workers led him to regard them as not true Communists.

After the defeat of Japan in 1945, the uneasy truce between the Kuomintang and the Communists broke down, despite efforts at conciliation by the United States, through its envoy, George C. Marshall. Civil war again erupted. The Kuomintang, exhausted by its long resistance to the Japanese and burdened by inefficiency and corruption, was quickly defeated. In 1949 it took refuge on Taiwan (Formosa) and neighboring islands. There the government of the Republic of China, which the Kuomintang controlled, was protected and aided by the United States. On the mainland no non-Communist group existed which was well organized and strong enough to take over the Herculean task of reconstruction after the years of foreign invasion and civil strife. It was to that task that the Communists resolutely addressed themselves.

The obstacles which the Communists faced in 1949 would have seemed insuperable to less confident men. The country was suffering from the aftermath of the Japanese invasion which had begun seventeen years before, in September, 1931. After the defeat of the Japanese in the summer of 1945 (an outcome of World War II due chiefly but not entirely to the Americans) China was exhausted by the long struggle. Runaway inflation ensued and a publicized effort by the Nationalists to check it ended in even more disastrous chaos. Under the stress of the war, transportation—notably that of the railways—had broken down. The beginnings which had been made in modern industry had suffered. Manchuria, where, thanks to the Japanese, industrialization and mining by up-to-date methods had proceeded furthest, had been largely stripped of its machinery: the Russians, moving in during the summer of 1945, had systematically taken to their own territory all that could conveniently be transported. China was predominantly rural. Famines had long been recurrent. Could the millions be lifted above the level of chronic undernourishment? The Communists were confronted by a world which was either suspicious or hostile: the Russians were as yet unconvinced that friendship with the Chinese Communists was to their interest; war still technically existed with Japan; the United States was openly critical; and the British were guarded in according recognition to the Communist regime.

Communist Assets

To offset the seemingly insuperable difficulties, the Communists could count on important assets. The overwhelming majority of the Chinese had completely lost whatever confidence they might have had in the Kuomintang, and they were prepared therefore to welcome strong leadership and the possibility of escape from their desperate plight. The Communists appeared to be the viable alternative to the discredited Nationalists. By long tradition the masses were resourceful and industrious, and among them were many men and women of outstanding ability. As we are to see, before the Japanese invasion, noteworthy progress had been made in a China which was adjusting itself to the incursion of the West, and given domestic and foreign peace, that progress could be resumed. Chinese intellectuals were intensely patriotic and would welcome leadership which would free the nation from the more than ten decades of humiliating subservience to the foreigner.

The Communists seemed to be capable of utilizing the assets. They had a convinced and disciplined leadership; despite internal dissensions, they presented a united front to the nation and to the world; no such spectacular purges troubled their ranks as had the

Russian Communists. The Chinese Communist Party was well organized and possessed a loyal and well-trained army. And Mao Tse-tung and his associates were convinced that in their program lay the country's salvation.

In 1949, the Communists at once began putting their program into effect concurrently pursuing several approaches.

The Indoctrination of the Nation

The Communists regarded as fundamental the indoctrination of the population in socialist ideals and methods. They were determined to bring the millions to an acceptance of the Communist ideology as Mao Tse-tung and his colleagues understood it. Now followed a prolonged effort at the most gigantic reshaping of a people that the world had ever seen. Nowhere else in human history had a regime undertaken as thorough a transformation of the basic conceptions of as many millions in so brief a time as the Communists attempted.

To this end the Communists employed a variety of methods. For the more influential elements, especially the openly or covertly dissident, they used what was called "brain-washing," or, more euphemistically, "thought reform." They required a purging of anti-Communist convictions, whether "bourgeois," "imperialist," or "capitalist," and indoctrination in the Communist ideals and interpretations of history and social structure. This entailed written confessions showing evidence of repentance and of acceptable conformity. For the more willing, lectures and discussions were conducted, with instruction in Marxism, self-examination, and correction by the group. The lectures and group discussions were routine features of schools, factories, and offices, and Marxist principles were an integral part of all education from kindergarten to university. Mass propaganda was spread through the radio, loud-speakers on trains and other places where the rank and file could be reached, and through placards, cartoons, movies, the theater, and popular fiction. Hatred of the United States as the alleged major enemy was insistently inculcated, partly as a means of promoting national solidarity behind the government. Membership in the Chinese Communist Party and armed forces entailed education in Marxism.

In the effort at full conformity, the Communists sought to curb all possible critics who had anti-Communist relations outside China. To this end they brought pressure on the Christians. Although they professed to hold to their constitutional guarantee of freedom of religious belief, the Communists were frankly atheistic and were intolerant of any ideological dissent.

All missionaries, Roman Catholic or Protestant, were charged with collaboration with foreign imperialists. Cited as damning evidence was the fashion in which treaties had been exacted at the mouth of cannon to include permission for missionaries to spread their faith and Chinese to accept it.

In 1949, Christians were small minorities—less than one in a hundred of the population. The Roman Catholics, who made up between two-thirds and three-fourths of the total, were in communion with the Papacy, which was emphatically anti-Communist. The Communists, therefore, required the Catholics to break their ties with the Vatican and they expelled or imprisoned all Roman Catholic missionaries. They encouraged the formation of a Patriotic Catholic Association and induced some Chinese bishops to consecrate others and thus continue the apostolic succession. The Vatican excommunicated adherents of the Association, and especially the bishops and clergy, while the Communists imprisoned or otherwise persecuted those who upheld the Vatican. Protestants were also subjected to pressure. All their missionaries were permitted to leave or were expelled and no financial assistance from abroad was allowed. Protestants were encouraged to form a national association that had for a slogan an ideal which had long been that of Protestant missions—self-support, self-government, and self-propagation. The extensive schools, hospitals, and other philanthropic institutions, most but not all of them connected with the Protestant churches, were taken over by the state. Under these circumstances the numbers of Christians declined. But in 1963 some conversions were still being made and baptisms were reported, both of adults and infants.

The Communists also attacked Buddhism. Although as a demonstration of religious tolerance to visiting foreign Buddhists they repaired a few temples, for the most part they applied principles of "land reform" to the holdings of Buddhist monasteries, and thus erased the endowments of these institutions. They required the monks and nuns to engage in what the Communists regarded as useful labor. However, they encouraged the formation of a Buddhist Association loyal to the state, and in 1963 the traditional pilgrimages to Buddhist sacred mountains persisted, though on a diminished scale.

To Taoism, much less vigorous than Buddhism, similar measures were applied. However, since Taoism, purely indigenous, had no foreign connections, few of its physical properties were preserved.

However, the Communists preserved and restored some Taoist and Buddhist structures as cultural monuments. In 1963 they sought to enlist Buddhists to protest the anti-Buddhist measures of the regime in South Vietnam. To obtain the cooperation of the adherents of Islam, another religion of foreign origin and with connections outside China, they stimulated the formation of the China Islamid Association, and aided the Chinese Institute of Islamic Theology for training Moslem scholars.

The success of the mass education cannot be accurately measured. Since livelihood and advance in the highly competitive society entailed conformity, the overwhelming majority complied. Millions did so from conviction or from inertia; exposure to alternatives was not permitted. Among thousands, possibly millions, self-interest was probably the dominant motive. Foreign visitors noted that they heard everywhere the same clichés in response to their questions. In 1956 the Communist leadership appeared to grant freedom of discussion and publicly said: "Let all flowers bloom and let diverse schools of thought contend." But so much criticism of the government was voiced during the "hundred flowers" period that in June, 1957, rigorous measures were taken against the "rightists."

Civil Strife and Foreign Invasion

The Communists set out to repair the economic damage done to the country by prolonged civil strife and foreign invasion. Immediately urgent were the problems of currency inflation and crippled transportation.

Like the Nationalists, the Communists insisted on a managed currency. They clamped down on the use of silver dollars, gold, and foreign currencies and instead issued their own paper money which they called the People's Currency (JMP). In 1954 they substituted for it a new JMP currency whose exchange rate with the old was 1 to 10,000, which they professed was based upon reserves of gold, silver, and foreign exchange. They attempted to restrict its issue to the People's Bank, a government institution, yet agricultural and producers' cooperatives printed notes of small denominations which had a wide circulation, especially in rural areas.

The Communists endeavored to cut down government expenditures, to give the central government control over provincial and local budgets, to fix prices, and to reduce the amount of money in

circulation by requiring the purchase of government bonds. For at
least some years they claimed that they had balanced the national
budget, but that budget mounted steeply.

The Communists rapidly repaired the tracks, rolling stock, and
bridges of the railroads. They cleaned and kept spotless the passenger
coaches, and—an innovation for much of China—had the trains
running on time. They built additional railways, some in the central
and coastal provinces, and much in the northwest. One line crossed
Mongolia to connect with the trans-Siberian and shorten the rail
distance to Europe. Another, across Sinkiang, had a junction with a
Russian line in Central Asia. A great bridge, long projected, was constructed across the Yangtze River at the urban center of Wuhan
and made possible for the first time direct rail service between Canton and Europe. Some double-tracking of main lines was undertaken.
Old highways were repaired and new ones were put through. Domestic and foreign air service, begun under the Kuomintang, was
stabilized and enlarged.

Early in the 1960's, however, critics were saying that in the railways much inefficiency existed, especially in the shipment of freight.
They declared that food needed in destitute regions was allowed to
accumulate and spoil, and that some raw materials were unpardon-
ably slow in reaching the factories to which they were assigned.

With his peasant background Mao Tse-tung was convinced that
the revolution must deal basically with agriculture and rural organization. As he and many of his colleagues saw it, Chinese utilization
of the land was suffering from a number of evils. Although far from
universal, landlordism and high rents were widespread; akin to this
were money debts, sometimes to the landlords, with burdensome
interest rates. Most cultivation was in small plots by intensive application of human labor; extensive use of labor-saving machinery and of
fertilizers was either impossible or difficult. During much of the
year, especially in the severe winters of the north, the soil could not
be worked and for months farmers were idle and potential labor was
lost.

Through a succession of steps the Communists endeavored to
eliminate these obstacles to the nation's livelihood. A policy of
"land reform" was promptly applied. It had earlier been employed
where the Communists were in control and it was now made nation-
wide. Landlords and moneylenders were eliminated and the acres
released were divided among the peasant cultivators. In the process,

public trials were held of the former owners and creditors, the populace was encouraged to voice grievances, and many of the accused were executed. The total number of victims could not be determined, but critics have estimated that it ran into the millions before "land reform" was pronounced completed in 1952.

"Land reform" was only the beginning. If agriculture was to provide the food for the labor in the industries which the Communists were determined to develop, and if such raw materials as cotton were to be grown in adequate supply, further organization appeared necessary. In 1953 the farmers were induced to join "mutual aid teams" which were transformed in 1954 into "agricultural producers' cooperatives" for the pooling of land, implements, draft animals, and labor. In 1956 the cooperatives were absorbed into "collective farms," some of them state-owned and others the joint property of the cultivators; in 1958 the government claimed that 95 per cent of farmers were in these "collectives" which were to make possible the use of tractors and other mechanical devices. "Communes," which superseded the "collective farms" in 1958, had common kitchens and mess halls; group care of infants, rearing of children; and feeding, clothing, and sheltering of the aged. By these measures, it was claimed, millions of women were freed from household tasks for labor in the fields and in rural industries, the soil could be cultivated in units on which machinery could be profitably employed, systematic irrigation and the economical use of fertilizers could be promoted, destructive pests could be eliminated, public health could be furthered by clinics and hospitals, and collective recreation could be aided. Local year-round industries, so the Communists declared, could be developed, thereby reducing seasonal unemployment. For a time peasants were encouraged to set up small plants for the smelting of iron; extensive projects for irrigation were undertaken; much needed reforestation of barren lands was initiated. Quotas for "cooperatives" and "communes" were fixed, and sale to the government was required. Much of the food thus obtained was resold to the urban population, assigned to officials, or exported to acquire foreign exchange and to repay Russian loans.

Reports of the effects of these measures varied. Some foreign travelers declared that they had seen much heartening local initiative. Critics said that the government had moved too fast, that on the whole peasants were reluctant to cooperate, that Communist Party cadres had shown ignorance of local conditions, that much of the irrigation had brought to the surface mineral salts which had reduced fertility and that frequently by disturbing the natural balance the campaigns against pests had aggravated rather than reduced the toll on the crops. They pointed to widespread undernourishment in the cities and to even worse conditions in rural areas. Early in the 1960's the government admitted shortages, and to offset them purchased grain in Canada and Australia, but it claimed that the deficiencies were due to an unprecedented series of natural disasters rather than to its program. By 1964 modifications in the "communes" were announced. The land was turned over to smaller groups, and the peasants were permitted to own land on which they could grow food and livestock for their use. By 1963 the worst of the immediate crisis had passed. Attempts were being made to tighten the commune system, but even in government circles these were being criticized and in 1964 complaints were voiced in the official press that some landlords and rich peasants were endeavoring to subvert cadres and workers in efforts to take over leadership.

The Population Problem

Basic to the problem of the supply of food and of such products of the soil as cotton was the mounting number to be fed and clothed. In 1920 estimates placed the population at between 350,000,000 and 428,000,000. In 1953 the official census said that on the mainland the total was 582,600,000. In 1961 the Communists declared that, including Taiwan, the population was 678,000,000. This appeared to be a spectacular increase, and an increase in spite of prolonged civil war and foreign invasion. The growth was accelerated by the Communist nation-wide campaign for public health and the consequent reduction in the death rate. The education of physicians and nurses was promoted, hospitals and clinics were multiplied, antibiotics were manufactured in quantity, and campaigns for vaccination against such diseases as smallpox and cholera were undertaken. Systematic attempts were made to take advantage not only of Western methods, but also of traditional Chinese practice; both medical systems were regarded as useful. Regular pauses for calisthenics were the rule in the schedules not only of schools but also of offices, and foreign travelers noted that at the first morning stops on long train trips passengers and attendants were encouraged through loud-speakers with music and instructions to join in athletic exercises. Early in the Communist regime campaigns were inaugurated to rid the cities of filth, flies, rats, and other pests, and in a number of urban centers considerable success was achieved.

To meet the increase in population, in March, 1957, a major nation-wide effort at birth control was launched, but before the end of the year it was discontinued. In 1962, however, the government began a campaign for the postponement of marriages, for planned families, and for familiarity with the use of contraceptives.

Yet these measures could not cope with the problem fully. During the acute food shortage late in the 1950's and early in the 1960's, some physicians left the mainland complaining that it was useless to combat disease in bodies undernourished and hence susceptible to infection.

Reorganization of Industry and Trade

True to their principles, the Communists early set about the nationalization of trade and industry. Some nationalization had been achieved under the Kuomintang, but in 1949 private ownership was the prevailing pattern. In the decade which followed 1949 the Communists took over almost all the trade and industry of the country, some in the form of joint managership by the former owners and the state, and the majority in state enterprises.

Beginnings had been made in industrialization before 1949, mostly by foreigners in Shanghai and especially by the Japanese in Manchuria. But prior to the Japanese invasion industrialization was still in its infancy. The Communists were determined to make the country as soon as possible one of the greatest industrial nations and purely under Chinese control. They boasted that in a very few years they would overtake Great Britain and eventually would surpass the United States in industrial production. They spoke of the rich coal and iron resources of China; they said that the geological surveys which they had initiated disclosed unsuspected vast deposits of iron and petroleum; and they pointed to enormous potentials of hydroelectric power, especially in the vast canyon through which the Yangtze pours its waters from the west to the lower reaches of its valley. The Huangho (Yellow River), only secondary in volume, breaks through gorges which would be suitable for dams for irrigation and power. The Communists could count on a supply of labor unmatched in size, traditionally inured to hard work, and unsurpassed in potential but as yet undeveloped skills.

In the realization of their dream of industrialization, they rehabilitated and enlarged the Japanese plants in Manchuria. In Peking they constructed factory after factory, and to accommodate the government offices, the thousands of laborers, and the new enterprises, they pierced the imposing city walls, improved and added to the streets, and erected apartment houses. Most of such industrialization as had existed had been on or near the coast, in touch with commerce from the West and Japan by way of the sea. Now an increasing proportion of the construction was in the northwest and Inner Mongolia.

Industrialization was pushed by a variety of methods. Much, together with the building of highways and railways, was by conscripted labor—reminiscent of what we shall see was an ancient and persistent Chinese tradition. Communists talked of "reform through labor" and consigned to such "reform" many from the dissident or doubtful elements of the population. They also insisted that all students and office workers vary their routine by manual labor in the fields, in construction, or in industry. They thus sought to abolish the traditional gulf between the intellectuals and manual laborers and to make good their ambition of a people's—or proletarian—society. Many students were said to "volunteer" for arduous projects in the northwest.

Labor was organized into unions. The unions were grouped into local, provincial, regional, and national federations. They were encouraged to promote in their members loyalty to the state and its purposes, to prevent waste and corruption, to maintain spare-time schools for their members, to conduct training schools for their officers, and to promote centers of recreation and culture. For the laborers provisions were made for health clinics, hospitals, medical care, and insurance against sickness, accidents, and old age.

Through five-year plans the Communists set goals. They also encouraged standards of production in individual industries. By rewards for exceeding quotas, by radio and loud-speakers, and by other propaganda methods they urged labor to put forth its full strength. Increasing numbers of women were employed, and hours of labor were long. "Voluntary" contributions for government bonds reduced wages, and yet wages were designed to enable the purchase of enough food to maintain health and efficiency, efforts were made at sanitary if not luxurious housing, and recreation was provided. In 1958 much was heard of the "great leap forward."

The Communists were aware that to maintain and improve the economy a working balance must be achieved between industry and agriculture. They talked of "walking on two legs"—by which they meant stressing both industry and agriculture.

Late in the 1950's communes also appeared in the cities. They were said to have developed largely through group initiative, in part by women. The urban communes were primarily administrative units and impinged much less on the daily life of the people than did their rural counterparts.

Much help was obtained from the Russians and other nations of the Communist bloc, partly in the form of machinery and largely as technical assistance. It decreased as the years passed, as additional machinery was constructed and as more Chinese technical experts were trained.

The vast food shortage of the early 1960's led to a sharp curtailment in industry. Much labor was diverted to agriculture, and in some regions the output of factories was said to have been reduced by three-fourths. Yet a determined effort was made to maintain the full production of iron and steel, and light industry to produce consumers' goods was encouraged.

Education

The Communists were aware that if their goals were to be attained, education must be made universal and vastly improved. Under the Republic of China remarkable advances had been achieved. The Communists sought to add to them, and they stressed literacy, as had the Republic of China. In 1960 they asserted that within the decade the literacy rate had been increased from 20 to 80 per cent of the population of school age and above. One objective was universal primary and secondary education for both sexes. Universities and higher technical institutions were multiplied. Part-time schools were conducted for workers; in 1960 the claim was made that each of the several counties of the country had at least one such school. Specialization was stressed in the natural sciences, medicine, agriculture, mining, engineering, foreign languages, and physical education. Russian was the foreign language most widely taught, but instruction in English, previously more popular, continued and later was emphasized at the expense of Russian.

Part of the program of every school was education in Communist ideals and physical exercises to promote bodily fitness.

As a result of the Communist educational system, millions of Chinese were being trained in one form or another of science as the modern West understood that term. Here and there fully competent and even distinguished scientists were emerging.

Students continued to go abroad in large numbers. Before the Communist regime, the overwhelming majority had gone to Japan, America, and Western Europe. But after 1949 and until late in the 1950's almost all went to Russia. For a time foreign students were encouraged to attend Chinese schools, especially in Peking.

Early in the 1960's, however, fewer Chinese went to Russia and as far as possible those who went kept strictly aloof from the Russians and Russian life. At the same time the number of foreigners studying in Peking sharply declined and those who came had difficulty in establishing personal contacts with Chinese.

In 1960-1962 a drastic reduction in the enrollment in secondary and higher schools was officially reported. This was ascribed to a lack of a sufficient number of well-trained teachers.

Language Reform

Years before the Communist triumph efforts had been made to further the union of the country by the universal use of one national language. Into the twentieth century many vernaculars had been spoken, and many of them, especially on the coast from Shanghai southward, were reciprocally unintelligible. However, throughout China, one form or another of what foreigners called Mandarin— the standard was supposed to be that of the capital, Peking—was understood. For many years the effort had been made through the schools to teach as the *kuo yü*, or "national language," a form of Mandarin that combined elements from various sections of the Mandarin-speaking areas, and thus would be accepted throughout the country. The Communists reinforced this program. For at least three decades before the Communist victory, many of the younger intellectuals had been writing in a dignified form of Mandarin. Previously all scholarly literature had been in a classical style which was quite different from the vernacular and which required special training to compose in an acceptable form, and even to read. The Communists emphasized composition in the non-classical form of written Chinese; they also adopted simplified forms of the characters.

Innovators though they were, the Communists endeavored to conserve the best of China's past as they interpreted it. They rewrote China's history in terms of Marxism-Leninism. They encouraged and subsidized archaeological research. New construction on historic sites and the extension of highways and railroads uncovered many ancient graves and remains of buildings and walls, and archaeologists were trained to take advantage of them for research purposes. In at least one instance, quite independent of other enterprises, a great imperial tomb was entered and its contents were preserved and put on public display. Although Confucianism as a cult was forbidden, some Confucian temples were repaired as artistic monuments of the past.

Remaking the Social Structure

A major feature of the Communist program was the revolutionizing of the social patterns of the nation's life. As we shall see, the greatest influence on pre-twentieth century Chinese culture was Confucianism. It was that ideology which governed the Chinese outlook and determined the features of Chinese society and state. Confucianism was perpetuated by the educational system, the state, and the family. Of these three bulwarks, before the Communists came to power, the first two had been undermined or swept aside. In the first decade of the twentieth century the civil service examinations based on the Confucian classics had been so profoundly altered that these writings, while not completely abandoned, had been relegated to a subordinate place in the curriculum. In 1911-1912 the Confucian monarchy had given way to the Republic of China. The Confucian traditional family system remained, but by 1949 it was being progressively weakened. Through it parents arranged for the marriages of their children, the primary loyalties were to the family, ethics were largely based on respect for parents and on family solidarity, the place of women was declared to be in the home, and the education given girls was designed to prepare them for domestic occupations. Many intellectuals had already rebelled against this. To the Communists the traditional family system was anathema, and they sought to abolish it.

Against the Confucian family the Communists took vigorous and comprehensive action. In the early days of their triumph they encouraged children to denounce their fathers as "reactionaries," "bourgeois," and enemies of the new socialist order. From the Confucian standpoint, this was a major crime. Historically the five human relationships stressed by Confucianism were those between father and son, younger brother and older brother, husband and wife, the prince and his minister, and friend and friend. Three, it will be seen, were within the family. In place of these five relationships, the Communists inculcated in children "five loves"—love for the motherland, for people, for work, and for knowledge, and respect for public property.

By these measures the Communists did not intend the destruction of the immediate family, but simply of the traditional family system. They encouraged youths to arrange their own marriages; they inculcated strict sexual morality and the subordination of sex to the welfare of the people as embodied in the state; they sought to abolish prostitution; the marriage law of 1950 forbade polygamy, child marriage, and infanticide; they regularized divorce and in their courts endeavored to persuade those contemplating that step to reconsider and if possible avoid it.

The Communists accelerated a development in the status of women which was already appearing. They put women in prominent positions in the state; they encouraged women to prepare for the learned professions and gave them employment in industry for the same wages as men; and the marriage law of 1950 gave property rights to women.

In other phases of their program the Communists sought to free the country of some of the chronic social ills of earlier days. They attempted to rid the cities of the beggars who were omnipresent in the old China. The rickshaw, devised in Japan by a foreigner and until 1949 characteristic of the cities, was replaced by the pedicab, presumably with less exploitation of unskilled labor. In the 1960's pedicabs were giving way to buses and automobiles.

The Political Structure

The Communist program was carried out through an inclusive political structure. Here the Communists did not completely sweep aside what had been inherited from the past. For the most part the historic geographic administrative units were preserved. That was true of the provinces and of the subdivisions of the provinces—except the *hsien*, a local unit roughly corresponding to the American county. The *hsien* were abolished, but later they were in part replaced by the communes.

Some other changes were effected. For example, modifications were made in the administration of what we might regard as non-Chinese peoples. The constitution declared that the People's Republic of China was a "unified, multinational state" and that "all the nationalities" were "equal." The overwhelming majority were "the Han

Chinese" or "the men of Han," a name from a dynasty that ruled the Empire for roughly four centuries immediately before and after the beginning of the Christian era. For some of the "non-Han" peoples the Communists recognized autonomous regions which in part represented pre-Communist geographic and racial divisions. The non-Han peoples were declared to be free to use their spoken and written languages and to preserve or reform their customs—but this liberty was not permitted to stand in the way of required conformity to the Communist pattern of socialism.

In general, as was to be expected, the structure of the People's Republic of China was profoundly influenced by that of the U.S.S.R. The Chinese Communist Party was in full control. At the outset it welcomed the cooperation of some non-Communist parties, but all of them were small and none was permitted to challenge the authority of the dominant party. In the period of the "blooming" of the "hundred flowers" some critics who spoke their minds were of the minority groups, but they were soon silenced or were brought to public confession and repentance of their "errors." They were not a serious menace. So secure did the leaders of the party feel that in 1959 official pardons were issued to high-ranking officers, civil and military, of the Republic of China who had been captured at the time of the Communist victory or had voluntarily cast in their lot with the Communists. Included in the list was Henry Pu-i, the last Emperor of the Manchu dynasty, who in the People's Republic became a gardener.

From time to time the leaders sought to alter the character of the membership of the Chinese Communist Party. In 1949 the membership was predominantly rural, partly because of a basic policy of Mao Tse-tung, and also because the areas controlled by the Communists were remote from large cities. In the 1950's more of the industrial proletariat were brought in; the party became more nearly representative of the nation as a whole. Efforts were made to purge unworthy elements from the membership, and a vigorous campaign was carried through of indoctrination through group meetings, self-criticism, and group criticism to eliminate cadres guilty of arrogance, graft, and lack of sympathy with peasants and laborers.

National congresses of the party were convened. The eighth, in 1956, with over a thousand delegates, adopted a revised constitution and confirmed the actions taken by the Central Committee and preparatory conferences. Provincial meetings of the party were also held, some of them for the first time in 1956. As large a body as the national congress could scarcely be deliberative; the real authority was not even in the Central Committee, but was exercised by a small Politburo and the latter's Standing Committee. That committee had six members, including Mao Tse-tung, Chou En-lai, Liu Shao-ch'i, and Chu Tê. In 1963 the chairman of the Chinese Communist Party was Mao Tse-tung.

The Chinese Communist Party was re-enforced by the Communist Youth League, the All-China Federation of Democratic Women, the All-China Federation of Trade Unions, the Young Pioneer Corps, the All-China Federation of Literary and Art Circles, the All-China Athletic Association, and the Chinese Science and Technology Association.

In 1954 the First National People's Congress adopted a constitution for the People's Republic of China. The drafting committee was chaired by Mao Tse-tung and had a Communist majority in its membership. The constitution stated that the People's Republic of China was a people's democratic state led by the workers and based on an alliance of workers and peasants. Citizens were guaranteed freedom of the press, freedom of assembly, freedom of demonstration, freedom of religious belief, freedom to choose and change their residence, privacy of correspondence, and inviolability of person and dwelling.

Under the constitution of 1954 the supreme authority was declared to reside in the National People's Congress and the local People's Congresses. The National People's Congress was the sole legislative authority. Its members were elected for four years by provinces, autonomous regions, municipalities directly under central authority, the armed forces, and overseas Chinese. It was to meet annually. Since the congress which convened in 1954 had 1,226 delegates, it could do little more than confirm measures proposed to it by its Standing Committee, a permanent body. Under the Standing Committee were the State Council, which might be called the executive branch of the government; the Supreme People's Procuratorate, which was supposed to serve as a censorate to safeguard the state and the party; the Supreme People's Court; and the National Defense Council. The Chairman of the Standing Committee was the titular head of the People's Republic of China. In 1964 he was Liu Shao-ch'i. The State Council had a premier, vice-premiers, and a number of ministries, commissions, and bureaus. In 1964 the premier was Chou En-lai.

In addition to the national government were ascending hierarchies of local and provincial governments. Each had its People's Congress, the members of which were elected by the next lower congress. Similarly at each stage the hierarchy included People's Courts and People's Procuratorates.

The constitution was frankly designed to be transitional and was intended to guide by successive stages progress from a capitalist to a socialist economy. No permanent code of laws was set up, but by 1960 several thousand criminal and basic statutes had been enacted. The professed purpose was the development of a legal system which would combine the best of ancient Chinese principles with the needs of an industrial society.

The Extension of Authority

The Communists endeavored to extend the authority and structure of the People's Republic of China to all the territory formerly embraced in the Empire. In its heyday, the last dynasty, that of the Manchus, officially bearing the name of Ta Ch'ing or Ch'ing, had ruled over more square miles than had any preceding dynasty. The Republic of China claimed this wide area and its maps pictured its boundaries as embracing it. It did not make its authority effective over all that it claimed, but in several regions it achieved progress. The People's Republic of China followed its example, and with mixed results.

No serious difficulty was encountered in Manchuria. Into that spacious region, with its vast natural resources of soil, minerals, and timber, in the earlier decades of the twentieth century the Han Chinese had poured by the million, and it was clearly theirs to control. Both the Russians and the Japanese had aspired to control it; the Japanese had been more nearly successful than the Russians. After 1945 the Republic of China had briefly held the main centers, but before 1949 the Communists had displaced them. To the People's Republic of China, as to the Republic of China, Manchuria was known as the Northeast, or the Northeastern Provinces. The Manchus, whose ancestral home it had been, were now a small minority. The People's Republic of China established its rule in the region more firmly than any central government of China had done since the collapse of the Manchu dynasty (1911-1912)—and even since 1898 when the Russians had moved in. But beyond making some protests the Communists made no effort to regain the thousands of square miles north of the Amur and east of the Ussuri which had been ceded to Russia in 1858 and 1860.

In Inner Mongolia the Communists seem to have been largely successful. That broad region immediately north of China proper has been traditionally Mongol. Semi-arid, its marginal rainfall varies from year to year. At times the precipitation has been sufficient to support cultivation, and Han Chinese, farmers by long experience, moved in. At other periods rainfall has declined and the climate favored the semi-nomadic, pastoral economy which was the Mongol tradition. The Republic of China had been acknowledged by much of the region and had sought to administer it through a provincial structure. But in the 1930's the Japanese challenged the Republic of China and endeavored to win the Mongol tribes. The Communists sought to reaffirm Chinese rule. They ingratiated themselves with the Mongols by enabling the latter to regain possession of the ashes of Genghiz Khan, the great Mongol conqueror of the twelfth and thirteenth centuries, which had been a source of contention between the Japanese and the Republic of China.

In Outer Mongolia the People's Republic was not so successful. Although under the Manchus that region had been part of the Empire, after the collapse of the Ch'ing dynasty Chinese authority had been tenuous. In 1911, with the proclamation of the Republic of China, Outer Mongolia had declared its independence, and a year later Russia recognized the autonomy of the region. In 1912 and 1915 Russia, China, and Outer Mongolia agreed to Chinese suzerainty in the area, and in 1919, in view of the Communists' power in Russia, by troops and diplomacy the Republic of China asserted its authority. However, two years after, Baron Ungern, an anti-Communist Russian, drove out the Chinese, and he in turn was expelled by the U.S.S.R. By a treaty of 1924 that regime recognized Outer Mongolia as "an integral part of the Republic of China," but in practice it regarded that section as autonomous and opened direct relations with it. In 1946 the Republic of China formally recognized the independence of Outer Mongolia, or called simply Mongolia. In 1950 a treaty between the U.S.S.R. and the People's Republic of China confirmed and guaranteed that independence. But the People's Republic of China gave financial aid and sent advisers to the government of Mongolia. In 1961 the United Nations recognized the full independence of Mongolia, but in such a manner that the country was clearly in the Russian orbit. It now was called the People's Republic of Mongolia. Early in 1964 Mongolia accused Peking of interfering in its domestic affairs and of distributing "subversive propaganda." It requested that Chinese workers who had begun to come in 1955 "to help in the country's socialist construction," be withdrawn. In April they were reported to be leaving.

In the great area of Sinkiang the People's Republic of China made more progress. Here it was following in the steps of the Republic of China. In spite of a pro-Russian movement in one section, the Republic of China had exercised partial control over much of the region. In doing so it had made extensive use of force. Racially Sinkiang was a mixture complicated by the history of centuries. A corridor to China proper, many peoples had made it their home. It was overwhelmingly Moslem, though Moslems were also numerous in parts of China proper, especially in the northwest. As had the Republic of China, the People's Republic of China encountered resistance to its control, but in general it succeeded in making its rule effective. Through mining, industries, and railroads it sought to develop the enormous natural resources of the area.

Tibet proved to be highly controversial. The Manchus had extended their dominion over that sprawling, high, mountainous tableland inhabited for centuries by adherents of one or the other of two kinds of Lamaistic Buddhism. Buddhist monks and monasteries were in control, with almost all the land held by the state, the monasteries, and the nobility. The peasant tenants' living was chiefly in herds and grain. So far as it had a central government, Tibet was under the Dalai Lama, a monk with his capital at Lhasa, and the less powerful Panch'an Lama, also a monk; the Manchus had recognized the Dalai Lama as the temporal ruler of the country. Early in the twentieth century Anglo-Russian rivalries drew Tibet into the net of world politics. In 1904 a British force fought its way to Lhasa and extracted a convention which provided for commercial relations and contained a Tibetan promise not to grant concessions without the consent of the United Kingdom. In 1906 Peking confirmed that agreement. The following year Russia and Britain recognized Chinese suzerainty in the country and promised that neither would seek concessions, but in 1912, upon the downfall of the Manchus, the Tibetans drove the Chinese troops from their territory and became practically independent. Two years later Great Britain, then still in control of India, entered into an agreement with Tibet that, among other terms, declared that the portion of Tibet bordering on India, while nominally under Chinese suzerainty, was to be practically autonomous.

The People's Republic of China sought to bring Tibet fully under its sway. In October, 1950, only a few months after achieving the mastery of the mainland, the Communists sent an army into Tibet to "liberate" its people and to "consolidate the national defenses of China's western corner." India, now a little over three years free from British rule and sensitive over the threat to its northern borders, formally protested the Chinese use of force. In reply, Peking declared Tibet to be an integral part of the territory of China and the hostilities to be purely a domestic affair of the People's Republic of China. In November, 1950, Tibet appealed to the United Nations, but the latter was estopped from action by the insistence of the U.S.S.R. and the Republic of China that Tibet was a part of China, and the following May Tibet formally accepted the suzerainty of the People's Republic of China.

In April, 1954, Peking and New Delhi seemed to have settled their differences by an agreement which permitted trade and cultural relations between India and Tibet, promised reciprocal nonaggression, noninterference in each other's internal affairs, and peaceful coexistence. The preceding December Peking had taken preliminary steps to create in Tibet a form of government more nearly in accord with Communist ideals. In March, 1959, resistance broke out into open revolt. The Dalai Lama fled to India to escape arrest by the Communists for his alleged complicity in the uprising. In the hostilities which were a part of the revolt, many Tibetans took refuge in India. However, the Communists induced the Panch'an Lama to come to Peking and in 1960 had him endorse their program of "land reform."

The struggle attracted the attention of much of the world. In October, 1959, the General Assembly of the United Nations formally deplored the Communist measures and called for respect for the fundamental human rights of the Tibetans. The following August a nongovernmental organization, the International Commission of Jurists, declared that in their attempt to destroy the Tibetans as a religious group the Communists were guilty of genocide and had violated the United Nations' declaration of human rights.

Undeterred, the People's Republic of China pursued its program.

It declared that by November, 1960, "land reform" had been accomplished; land, draft animals, tools, and dwellings belonging to owners who had not joined in the revolt had been purchased by the state; property of those who resisted had been confiscated; and all had been distributed among the peasants. Peking claimed that the former "serfs" had been "awakened," that a vast "movement for production in agriculture and animal husbandry had been set in motion," and that "the broad masses of the laboring people," who had become free, had "reaped the greatest harvest in farm produce and stockbreeding in Tibet's history."

Macao and Hong Kong, once integral parts of China, remained in foreign hands. To the present, the Communists have made no effort to take possession. On a small peninsula of an island near the important southern port of Canton, since the latter part of the sixteenth century Macao has been ruled by the Portuguese, and is now of slight commercial or political importance, but has been a door of escape for many Chinese unhappy under the Communist regime.

Except for the Japanese occupation (December, 1941–August, 1945), part of Hong Kong has been in British hands since 1842 and the remainder through a ninety-nine-year lease dating from 1898. As a British colony Hong Kong has prospered. It is predominantly Chinese in population, and has long been important as a commercial port. After the Communists took over the mainland, hundreds of thousands of refugees from Communist territories found asylum in Hong Kong and by 1964 the population had risen to more than 3,000,000. Some of the refugees were wealthy, but the large majority were poverty-stricken and their livelihood, housing, and education constituted a major problem. To it the British authorities valiantly have addressed themselves, assisted by nongovernmental philanthropic agencies, chiefly but not entirely from the British Commonwealth and the United States. The British authorities have been careful to maintain strict neutrality between the Communists and the non-Communists, and Peking has been content to observe the status quo, presumably because it has found Hong Kong convenient for economic contact with the non-Communist world. Through growing industries, commerce, and tourism Hong Kong has prospered.

Adventure in Korea

The Communists engaged in a notable adventure in Korea. For many centuries that peninsula had been within the Chinese sphere of influence, much of its culture had come from China, and from time to time part or all of it had been politically within the Chinese Empire. Under the Manchus, Korea had acknowledged China as its suzerain. Not until 1895, as a result of a war with Japan, had China recognized the independence of the country. As an aftermath of that war, Japan increased its influence and formal annexation came in 1910, but as a result of World War II, Japan was forced to withdraw. The Russians moved into the North (above the 38th parallel) and the Americans into the South, both ostensibly to implement the Japanese surrender. In their zone the Russians set up a Communist government, while south of the thirty-eighth parallel, at the instance of the United States, the United Nations, through a temporary commission, created the Republic of Korea. The General Assembly of the United Nations declared that the Republic of Korea had been based on the wishes of the Koreans expressed through free elections. The United Nations recognized the regime as the legitimate government for all Korea, but the Russians would not permit it to include the North, and they and their satellites held that the government in the North should rightfully control all the country. In June, 1950, North Koreans, equipped with Russian arms and declaring that they had been attacked by the South Koreans, crossed the thirty-eighth parallel and quickly overran most of the South. At the instance of the United States, the Security Council of the United Nations (which the Russians were temporarily boycotting) demanded that North Korea withdraw its forces and called on the member states to enforce the order. The main United Nations' contingents were provided by the United States, but several other governments also contributed men and matériel. By the end of the year they had pushed the Northern armies back almost to the Yalu River, the boundary between Korea and Manchuria.

The People's Republic of China, insisting that its territory was threatened and that Americans had used planes to scatter poison germs and to drop bombs on Manchuria, sent in thousands of troops, whom they described as "volunteers." They chose to ignore the participation of other members of the United Nations and declared that the United States was the "aggressor." By intense propaganda they whipped up public opinion on the mainland to "resist America, aid Korea." They appealed to the United Nations, but on February 1, 1951, the General Assembly of that body declared the People's Republic of China to be the aggressor. On July 27, 1953, an armistice was signed. It fixed the boundary, presumably temporarily, between the contending armies roughly at the thirty-eighth parallel. Prisoners were permitted to choose whether they would return home or accede to the other side. Hundreds of the Chinese and North Koreans decided against returning to their homelands, and only a few of the United Nations' men elected to remain with the Communists. From time to time, under the provisions of the armistice, conversations have been held on the neutralized border between the two zones on various issues and on the possibility of a peace, but into 1964 no agreement had been reached.

Although the decision of the forces of the United Nations not to press across the Yalu River into Manchuria seems to have been due not to military weakness but to President Truman's fear that the step might provoke the U.S.S.R. to enter openly into the conflict and so precipitate World War III, the Chinese Communists interpreted it as determined by the success of their "volunteers." To them the United States was "a paper tiger." They boasted that for the first time in history a Chinese army had defeated, in open battle, a major army of Westerners. Here was balm to the pride, not only of Chinese Communists, but of other Chinese as well, who had smarted under the many humiliations inflicted by Westerners on China in the nineteenth and twentieth centuries.

In North Korea, as in Mongolia, a thinly veiled conflict was seen between Moscow and Peking. Peking made substantial financial contributions to the North Korean regime. In 1964, and for the past several years, pro-Peking leadership was dominant, and the head of the North Korean government has joined with the People's Republic of China in denouncing the policies of Moscow.

The Southeastern Border

The People's Republic of China has been active in aiding Communism in Southeast Asia also where several Chinese dynasties had once exercised control. As early as the third century before Christ, Chinese rule had been extended to Annam and intermittently across the centuries parts of that area had been part of the Empire. From late in the eighteenth century until the last quarter of the nineteenth century, Annam had had a relationship with the Ch'ing dynasty resembling that of Korea. But at the outbreak of World War II Annam was included in what was known as French Indo-China, for, beginning in the eighteenth century, France had built up a colonial empire in the region, either by direct annexation or in the form of protectorates. French Indo-China included Tongking, Annam, Laos, Cambodia, and Cochin-China. During World War II the region was occupied by the Japanese, and after that struggle, France endeavored to regain its former position, but was met by the wave of anti-colonialism and anti-imperialism which was eliminating European control in most of Asia and Africa. The chief force in driving out the French was communism. The Vietminh, for instance, a Communist party founded and headed by Ho Chi Minh and aided by Chinese Communists, in 1954 defeated the French.

In 1954 at a conference in Geneva dealing with both French Indo-China and the Korean issues, Chou En-lai, the chief representative of the People's Republic of China, attempted to dominate the meeting. In addition to arriving at the armistice in Korea, the Geneva gathering effected a settlement in the French possessions in Southeast Asia. By it French rule was canceled, Laos and Cambodia were declared neutral, and the rest of the territory was divided between North Vietnam, controlled by the Vietminh, and South Vietnam, a republic under a devout Roman Catholic layman, Ngo Dinh Diem, a bachelor. Neither the United States nor Ngo Dinh Diem subscribed to the Geneva settlement of the problems of Southeast Asia.

As in Korea, so in Southeast Asia, the Geneva Conference brought about an uneasy truce rather than lasting peace. With the support of Peking, Communist infiltration sought to gain the upper hand in both Laos and South Vietnam. Peking gave extensive financial aid to North Vietnam. When, in 1962, the United States sent help to South Vietnam, Peking protested that the American military assistance jeopardized the peace of the Far East. In the summer of 1962, after long negotiations at Geneva, an agreement over Laos was reached which, among other terms, promised the withdrawal of foreign troops from that unhappy country.

A commission composed of representatives of Canada, India, and Poland to which the supervision of the 1954 armistice was entrusted was also charged with the responsibility of seeing that the 1962 accord was observed. Communist troops persisted in encroaching on the neutral territory. In May, 1963, the U.S.S.R., unhappy over Peking's activity in the region but reluctant to intervene too vigorously, was induced by Great Britain to seek to bring adherence to the 1962 document.

In 1963 Buddhist protests threatened the regime in South Vietnam, and in November of that year a military revolt swept it out of power. Ngo Dinh Diem and his brother were murdered. In the first half of 1964 the successor government was unstable. In Laos domestic strife augmented by Communist forces from North Vietnam mounted. Peking, openly sympathetic with the insurgents, vigorously denounced the United States.

In addition to its activities in Vietnam and Laos the People's Republic of China made its weight felt in other parts of South and East Asia and the adjacent islands. Millions of Chinese were living in the Philippines, in North and South Vietnam, and in Malaysia, Thailand, Cambodia, British Borneo, Indonesia, and Burma. The largest contingents were in Singapore, Indonesia, and Thailand. Among all of them Peking endeavored to win support. In this it was continuing the policy of the Republic of China, for the latter had sought to place the Chinese in these regions under its protection. Communist propagandists were active, notably in the predominantly Chinese Singapore.

The Indonesian government found the Chinese in its territories an economic problem, for they monopolized much of the local trade. In 1954 a treaty between Peking and Jakarta sought an adjustment by requiring Chinese residents to choose between Indonesian citizenship and allegiance to the People's Republic of China. In 1959 difficulties arose over the effort of the Indonesian government to exclude the Chinese from the retail trade within its borders. In the 1960's a Communist party (Partai Komuni Indonesia) was active in Indonesia, led by Dipa Nusantro Aidit, who tended to follow Mao Tsetung in the latter's interpretation of Marx-Leninism. The situation was complicated by riots against the Chinese, evidence of long-standing resentment nurtured by what was deemed the Chinese exploitation of the Indonesians. Many of the Chinese had back of them generations of residence in the country, but the feelings against them were strong.

For some years after World War II and the restoration of British rule in Malaya, Communist guerrillas, most of them Chinese, harassed the countryside. By skillful and persistent measures the British subdued them before Malaya became independent in 1957.

In 1960 Peking entered into treaties of peace and friendship with Burma, Nepal, and Afghanistan. The treaty with Burma settled a border dispute and entailed concessions by both countries. Another treaty sought to define the boundaries between China and Nepal.

In 1963 Peking constructed a road to connect Tibet and Nepal. Under the Ch'ing, both Burma and Nepal, but not Afghanistan, had recognized the suzerainty of China. Many centuries earlier Chinese armies had penetrated what is now the mountainous north of Afghanistan which has an ill-defined border with Sinkiang. The treaty of 1960 did not define the boundary, but merely contained a reciprocal promise of respect for each other's independence, sovereignty, and territorial integrity.

With India pronounced friction developed and has continued to the present. In the earlier years of the People's Republic of China, efforts were made by both Peking and New Delhi to establish friendly relations, but friction was latent. In India, Communists were seeking control and were aided by the Chinese Communists. Both New Delhi and Peking aspired to the leadership of South and East Asia, but at an Asian-African conference in Bandung (1955), by the charm which he could exude, Chou En-lai achieved for his government the prominence which Nehru hoped to gain for the Republic of India. Peking regarded New Delhi not as neutral in the "cold war" as it professed to be, but as aligned with the enemies of communism. In 1959 the haven granted by India to the Dalai Lama and other Tibetan refugees further irritated Peking, and the mastery of Tibet by Peking was quickly followed by the dispatch of Chinese Communist troops into the Tibetan-Indian border. India moved forces into the disputed areas, and in 1962 hostilities broke out, primarily in Ladakh, which is on the northern frontier of Kashmir, a state to which the Indian claim was a chronic source of friction with Pakistan and the United Nations. Peking also considered this territory valuable because of important trade routes from Sinkiang to Inner Asia. India held to what was called the MacMahon Line, a boundary between Tibet and India drawn by a British official before Indian independence, but to which neither the Republic of China nor the People's Republic of China had agreed. In the autumn of 1962 Peking moved troops into the northeast border of India and threatened both Bhutan and Assam. Aid to India was given by the U.S.S.R., the United States, Great Britain, and Canada, and in November, 1962, Peking ordered its troops to cease fire and to make a partial withdrawal from the disputed areas, but did so on terms which were not acceptable to India. In December, 1962, representatives of six neutral nations—Ghana, Egypt, Indonesia, Burma, Cambodia, and Ceylon—met in Colombo and formulated a proposal for a settlement to which Peking has not agreed. In the autumn of 1963 Chou En-lai and Ch'en Yi visited Ceylon to attempt to win that country to their side, but failed. Peking's friendly agreements with Pakistan in 1963 further antagonized India.

The vigor with which the People's Republic of China was pushing its interests in Southeast Asia was arousing antagonism in several countries, and by 1963 the good impression made by Chou En-lai in Bandung was canceled by the fear of an aggressive Chinese imperialism, a fear which in India and in some other lands as well was mounting. In 1963 an agreement among Indonesia, the Philippines, and Malaya seemed to be evidence of their common concern. However, the emergence of Malaysia late in 1963 and the ensuing friction between that nation and Indonesia and the Philippines distracted attention from the menace to the North.

The People's Republic of China and the U.S.S.R.

Relations with the U.S.S.R. had a high place in the foreign affairs of the People's Republic of China, because both were Communist, because of the extended land frontier—the longest on the globe—between the two powers, and because of the pre-Communist importance of Russia in Chinese affairs, but relations were far from uniform and varied from coolness to ostensibly warm friendship and then to renewed coolness.

From late in the 1920's until 1949 the attitude of the U.S.S.R. toward the Chinese Communist Party was, if not openly unfriendly, decidedly lukewarm. After the 1920's, with the failure of the Communists to control the Kuomintang, the break with Chiang Kai-shek, and the split in the Chinese Communist forces, Stalin seemed to have written off the Chinese Communists. As we have suggested, the insistence of Mao Tse-tung on basing the revolution on the peasants rather than on the industrial proletariat was regarded by Stalin as unorthodox. In the early 1940's Stalin assured visiting American envoys that he believed the Republic of China to be of more use in resisting the Japanese than Mao Tse-tung and the others in Yenan, and though they left Japanese arms where the Chinese Communists could make use of them, in 1945 Russian troops stripped Manchuria of all the machinery which they could transport to the U.S.S.R.

In 1950 Moscow changed its policy, and in February, after prolonged negotiations which seem to have implied hard bargaining, a thirty-year pact of friendship between the People's Republic of China and the U.S.S.R. was made public. By it both signatories agreed to respect the sovereignty and territorial integrity of the other, and to come to each other's assistance in case of aggression by Japan if Japan was supported by an ally. The latter provision was a thinly veiled threat to the United States, for Japan and the latter were now closely associated. Additional terms of the settlement provided for a return to China of the Manchurian railways when a peace treaty with Japan had been concluded (or at the latest by the end of 1952); stated that the administration of Dairen was to be solely under the People's Republic of China; promised the withdrawal of Russian troops from Dairen and Port Arthur by December, 1952 (subsequently extended to May, 1955); and assured (U.S.) $60 million credits by Moscow for the purchase of materials from the U.S.S.R., to be repaid in raw materials, food, tea, gold, and American dollars. In explanation of the provisions concerning Dairen and Port Arthur it may be noted that in 1898 Russia had obtained a lease on the former, the chief port of Manchuria, and on the latter, a fortified post; as a result of her war with Japan (1904-1905) she had been forced to cede them to that country; and in August, 1945, in a treaty with the Republic of China, the U.S.S.R. had been given a favored position in Dairen and was permitted to defend Port Arthur, but with the joint use of that port with the Republic of China.

In October, 1949, a Sino-Soviet Friendship General Association was announced, which by 1951 claimed a membership of sixteen million in China. Throughout the mainland, pictures of Stalin and Mao Tse-tung were prominently displayed side by side, numbers of Russian technicians came as advisers to the Chinese, and the U.S.S.R. sent airplanes and munitions to assist the Communist "volunteers" in their resistance to the United Nations in Korea.

In 1954 Moscow deemed the friendship of Peking to be of sufficient importance to send a delegation to that city rather than, as in 1949-1950, to treat a deputation of Chinese Communists as suppliants. In the negotiations which ensued, Moscow agreed to deliver to Peking by January 1, 1955, its installations in the Port Arthur enclave and its share in the joint Sino-Soviet development companies which had given the U.S.S.R. a hold in China that was galling to Chinese nationalism, made hypersensitive by the Western aggression of the nineteenth and twentieth centuries.

Partially in return, as evidence that it deemed itself as an equal in Sino-Soviet relations, and perhaps also because it regarded itself as threatened by repercussions in its own territories, the People's Republic of China came pronouncedly to the support of the U.S.S.R. in the uprisings of 1956 in Hungary and Poland. To assure vividly the solidarity of Peking with Moscow, Chou En-lai interrupted a visit in Burma to fly to Warsaw and Budapest.

It must be noted that even at the height of the Sino-Soviet friendship Russia did not give atomic arms to the People's Republic. Moreover, the total monetary assistance of the U.S.S.R. was not impressive and was accorded only for a *quid pro quo* which must have proved an embarrassing drain on Peking's overburdened food resources.

Beginning in 1956 strains developed between Peking and Moscow. All of the causes are not known, but chief among them was the growing self-importance of the Chinese Communists. In accord with the conviction long cherished by the Chinese that they have been the exponents of the highest civilization, the leaders of the People's Republic of China regarded themselves as the only true interpreters of Marxism-Leninism. They agreed with Lenin that Marxist theory was flexible and must be adapted to changing conditions but insisted that theirs was the authentic understanding. Unlike the Communist régimes in Central Europe, they had come to power quite independent of Russian support. They therefore felt free to differ with Moscow. Outwardly they concurred with Khrushchev's denigration of Stalin, but they esteemed Mao Tse-tung rather than Khrushchev as the exponent of orthodox communism and openly disagreed with Khrushchev's insistence that the world-wide victory of communism could be achieved without war. As a symbol of their dissent they supported the Communist regime in Albania and in doing so openly ran counter to Khrushchev.

By 1964 no decisive rupture had occurred between Moscow and Peking. Efforts were made on both sides to present a common front to the world, but friction was inevitable and continued since each aspired to lead global communism. Rivalries between China and Russia long ante-dated the Communist capture of both realms, for as far back as the seventeenth century the Manchus had clashed with the eastward expansion of the Tsar's domains. At the time the victory rested with the Manchus. But with the growing deterioration of the Manchus, again and again in the nineteenth and the first decade of the twentieth century the gains had gone to the Russians. To the ill-concealed annoyance of Moscow, the People's Republic of China sought to dominate East and South Asia, as demonstrated at the Bandung Conference of African and Asian powers. In 1962, as we have said, Russia gave help to India when the latter was engaged in border hostilities with the People's Republic of China. By 1963 the People's Republic of China was clearly seeking to draw North Korea into its sphere at the expense of Russian aspirations which went back into the nineteenth century. The recognition by the United Nations in 1961 of the independence of Mongolia was a victory for Russia, for it was due to Russian diplomacy that that country was drawn into closer association with the U.S.S.R. In 1962 Peking criticized Moscow for yielding to the United States in promising to withdraw its missiles from Cuba; in 1963-64 the officially inspired Peking press accused Moscow of violating agreement after agreement with the People's Republic of China and hinted that the territory north of the Amur and east of the Ussuri, ceded to Russia in the mid-nineteenth century, should be returned. Peking alleged that Moscow had not fulfilled a promise made in 1957 to supply it with fissionable material and the atomic bomb. It declared that in 1960 the U.S.S.R. had withdrawn its technicians with their blueprints and had thus slowed the industrialization of China. It complained that Russia had demanded payment for its help, but said that by 1965 all its debts to that country would be repaid. It denounced the test ban treaty of 1963 between the U.S.S.R. and the United States and said that the two powers were plotting jointly to dominate the world. It also charged Russia with slowing the revolt against colonialism and imperialism in Asia, Africa, and Latin America, and held that Russia was becoming "bourgeois" and was aligning itself with the "have" against the "have not" peoples. Peking announced that it was calling an Africa-Asia conference in 1965, and, in spite of the U.S.S.R.'s protest that it was an Asiatic power, declared that the Russians belonged with the "white" peoples and would not be invited. The tensions were aggravated by personal tensions between Mao Tse-tung and Khrushchev. Moscow said that Peking was trying to deify Mao Tse-tung and that it was departing from the Marxism-Leninism which it professed to champion and that it was becoming Trotskyite—anathema to all true Communists. It also charged Mao Tse-tung with ruling illegally.

The Moscow-Peking rift was extending to the Communist parties of the world. In 1964 Moscow claimed that two-thirds were on its side, but pro-Peking factions were developing in many Communist parties in Europe and Latin America as well as in Asia.

Some attempts were made to heal the breach. In the Spring of 1964, a Rumanian delegation to China seems to have sought to bring the rivals together. In April, 1964, Moscow denied that it was trying to isolate Peking. In that month Peking sent hearty congratulations to Khrushchev on his seventieth birthday.

To the People's Republic of China the United States of America has been the outstanding enemy. Aggrieved by the support accorded by the Americans to the Republic of China in the interval between 1945 and 1949, they called attention to the arms then given the Republic of China and held America responsible for the death of many Communists. They consider American aid to what they refer to as the "Chiang Kai-shek clique," or "the Chiang Kai-shek bandits" which kept them from "liberating" Taiwan, to be wanton interference in China's civil war and the internal affairs of their country. They regarded the resistance of the United Nations to the North Koreans as due primarily to the government of the United States, and regard the United States as the chief opponent to the Communist advance in Southeast Asia. Here they could call attention to the South East Asia Treaty Organization as an alliance initiated and supported by the United States to check communism in that area. They also attribute to the United States the lack of recognition of the People's Republic of China by many countries; the opposition to the admission of that government to the United Nations; and the denial to Peking of the permanent seat held by China on the Security Council of that body. Washington, they point out, has attempted to shut them off from much of the commerce of the world. The United States forbids its citizens to trade with the People's Republic of China, cuts off treasury connections, and refuses passports to virtually all Americans who wish to travel in the territories controlled by the People's Republic of China. The United States, the Chinese Communists insist, has been the outstanding obstacle to the triumph of communism in the world at large. In spite of official efforts of the United States to ease the continued tension, Peking was emphatic that unless Washington abandoned its support of the Republic of China, no accomodation was possible.

However, diplomatic contacts with the United States have not been completely discontinued. Neither government gave *de jure* recognition to the other. But both governments were represented at the Geneva negotiations over Korea, Vietnam, and Laos. At Warsaw the ambassadors of the two powers have had hundreds of conversations on various issues, including the release of Americans held prisoner by Peking and possible American support to the Republic of China in its attempt to regain the mainland. In both the People's Republic of China and the United States, misinformation and lack of information about the other have been rife. Even the educated in the People's Republic of China have been convinced that wide unemployment and starvation exists among the American "proletariat." Americans have been somewhat better informed but are inclined to credit the more somber reports which have come from refugees and critics of the Communist regime.

In its support of the Republic of China and its opposition to the recognition of the People's Republic of China and of the latter's admission to the United Nations, until 1962 United States policy increasingly ran contrary to the opinion of the rest of the non-Communist world. As we have seen, the hostilities between India and the People's Republic of China caused several nations to regard the latter as an imperialistic aggressor and to vote against its admission to the United Nations. On January 27, 1964, France gave formal recognition to the People's Republic of China, and in April and May, 1964, exchanged ambassadors, after first forcing a severance of relations with France by the Republic of China. France came out for the admission of the People's Republic of China to the United Nations. In the spring of 1964 many conjectured that enough governments, especially of the French Community, would follow France's example to bring about admission.

The People's Republic of China and Japan

The People's Republic of China has regarded the United States as the major handicap to the establishment of peace and commercial relations with Japan. In May, 1952, Japan entered into a treaty of peace with the Republic of China in which it renounced all claims to Taiwan and the Pescadores. Peking could not but view as an affront the recognition of what it declared to be a rebel regime; for Japan's recognition it held the United States responsible.

From the standpoint of Japan, Peking's alliance with Moscow was dangerous. Japan had long viewed the Russian advance in East Asia as a menace and in 1904-1905 had fought a war to check it. The Japanese could not easily forget the Russian entrance into World War II in spite of the nonaggression pact of 1941 with that power, nor could they forget that when Japan was forced to its knees by the

United States, Russia came in for the easy kill and seized the Kurile Islands and the southern part of Sakhalin. By 1964 no peace had been concluded between Moscow and Tokyo. Officially the war had ended, but no agreement had been reached on territorial issues. Among other handicaps, the U.S.S.R. objected to the alliance of Japan with the United States and the presence of American troops and air craft on Japanese soil, regarding them as a threat to its Asiatic littoral. In this the People's Republic of China concurred.

Some efforts were made by Japanese and the Chinese Communists to renew commercial relations, since each would find the markets of the other of economic advantage. In 1958 such slight commerce as existed between Japan and the Chinese mainland was abruptly interrupted: a drunken Japanese tore down a flag of the People's Republic of China, Peking angrily demanded that its flag be respected when displayed in Japan, and cut off all trade until what it deemed adequate amends had been made. In contrast, a large proportion of the trade of the Republic of China was with Japan. Japanese youth and the Japanese Socialists tended to be impatient with the minimal contacts with the People's Republic of China and advocated the renewal of relations. But many merchants were fearful that if trade was resumed the People's Republic of China might interrupt it abruptly at any time and so bring loss to the Japanese involved.

Peking's Influence on the World Scene

The People's Republic of China was not content with making its weight felt only in East and Southeast Asia. It also was vigorous in seeking to promote communism on all the continents.

In Western Asia and North Africa, Peking was active. In 1956 diplomatic relations were established with Egypt and a trade agreement was signed and cultural exchanges were begun. In the Suez crisis (1956) Peking gave more support to Nasser than did Moscow, and after the British government had frozen Egypt's account in the Bank of England, Peking made its sterling assets available to Nasser. Peking also offered to send "volunteers" to Nasser. During 1957-1958 Peking entered into diplomatic relations with Yemen, Sudan, Iraq, Morocco, and Syria. In 1959 at the risk of a rupture with Nasser, Peking encouraged a Communist leader in Syria in a proposal that that country should withdraw from the United Arab Republic and join forces with the pro-Communist regime in Iraq. But as the Communist trend in Iraq waned, Peking's attitude toward Baghdad cooled. In 1958 the People's Republic of China became the first non-Arab state to recognize the Provisional Government of the Algerian Republic, and in spite of its own internal difficulties, in 1962 it promised medicine, steel, and wheat to help relieve the distress in the newly independent Algeria.

Peking has been quick to give recognition to the African nations which were obtaining independence from European colonialism. To some it has contributed concrete assistance: to Guinea economic and technical aid in rice-growing was given; in Ghana in 1961 Peking set up an exhibit to display progress achieved in various aspects of its industry. In general, in 1964 the Communists in several African countries were looking to Peking rather than to Moscow, presumably because they were suspicious of the latter's imperialistic designs. That attitude had been cultivated by Chou En-lai in a visit to Africa in the autumn of 1963. However, the Republic of China was also wooing the African states by sending experts to help improve the yields of rice and other agricultural products and by offering advice on industrialization.

Visitors from Latin American states have been cordially welcomed in Peking. Peking joined with Moscow in recognizing Castro's regime in Cuba and has offered it concrete assistance.

In Europe Peking has not only endorsed the radical Communist government in Albania, but has also been more consistently outspoken than Moscow in the denunciation of Tito and Yugoslavia for their deviation from what Peking regarded as orthodox Marxism.

Active though it has been in endeavoring to spread its interpretation of communism throughout the world, the People's Republic of China has in part resumed the isolationist policy which had characterized the Empire before the latter half of the nineteenth century. For example, in spite of de jure recognition by the United Kingdom, in 1963 the British embassy in Peking did not have an ambassador, the Chinese embassy in England was without a similar official, and consular relations were either absent or exiguous. Travel of diplomatic staffs in Peking on the mainland has been restricted and closely supervised. In many ways the Chinese of the mainland have been cut off from contact with the rest of the world and have heard only so much of events outside their borders as the regime has permitted and then merely from such angles as has suited the government. The Communists are intent on achieving and maintaining the solid support of their public.

To some degree this self-conscious and deliberate aloofness has been due to the hostility of the United States, the lack of membership in the United Nations, and the fact that Peking has still been branded by the United Nations as the aggressor in Korea and technically is still at war with that body. But the aloofness cannot be entirely attributed to these circumstances. Much stems from the conviction of cultural superiority which long had characterized the Chinese.

Peking was not included in the prolonged discussions on disarmament conducted under the auspices of the United Nations and has declared that it will not be bound by agreements on that vital issue in which it has not been consulted. Presumably Peking will in time develop atomic weapons. In 1962 it possessed the fourth largest submarine fleet—next after the U.S.S.R., the United States, and Great Britain.

As expected, the foreign commerce of the People's Republic of China has been chiefly with its fellow Communist bloc nations, but it also has had trade with countries outside that circle. By the mid-1950's it was exporting to neutrals in the power struggle between Communists and non-Communists and to some countries which were in alliance with vigorously anti-Communist lands. Among the exports were cotton textiles, machinery, tools, silk, and chemicals. With Ceylon rice was exchanged for rubber. From India came industrial products and tobacco. Indonesia supplied rubber, copra, timber, coconut oil, and sugar. In 1963 and 1964, because of the mounting strains with the U.S.S.R., trade with that country and with the Russian satellites in Europe fell off sharply.

Unrest

By 1964, as we have suggested, internal difficulties were besetting the People's Republic of China. Food was in short supply. As we have seen, Peking attributed the deficiency chiefly to a succession of natural calamities and sought to ease the situation by the purchase of wheat in Canada and Australia. It moved some of the urban population to the rural areas to augment the farm labor, and it modified the "communes" to encourage the peasants to greater productivity. Presumably in an effort to block off the Chinese from foreign criticisms and to keep the outer world in ignorance of the internal distress, so far as possible, as we have noted, Peking has kept Chinese students in Russia from contacts with non-Chinese. The number of foreign students in Peking has declined, and those who remained have found the cultivation of fellowship with Chinese students increasingly difficult. The boasts of the 1950's of industrial progress were muted. In at least some cities beggars reappeared and sanitary conditions deteriorated. Critics declared that the intense pressure to achieve industrial progress has brought widespread psychological and physical fatigue. Reports reached the outer world of unrest in the army, of corruption among Party cadres, and of numerous bands of guerrillas. Refugees seeking haven in Hong Kong have spoken of mounting undernourishment, infant mortality, and disillusionment. Whether these reports have distorted the picture cannot be ascertained. That the People's Republic of China has not fully solved the staggering problems which confronted it in 1949 is clear. Wide undernourishment has existed, but famine such as China had previously known, with millions dying of starvation, is not seen.

In the 1960's non-Communist foreign visitors who had been familiar with the China of the earlier part of the century were impressed with the vast improvement which the People's Republic had achieved. They noted the spectacular progress in industrialization; the advance in public health; the reduction of filth; the maintenance of order; the fact that the police were unarmed and appealed to reason rather than force; the reduction of corruption, graft, gambling, and organized vice; the unfailing courtesy; and the clean, well-fed, and well-clothed children in contrast with the rags and dirt of millions in an earlier day. They remarked on the pride of the Chinese in the achievements under the Communist regime in domestic and foreign affairs. At long last, after the humiliations and distresses of more than a century, the Chinese, non-Communist as well as Communist, could feel pride in their country. Yet visitors also reported that the price of these achievements has been sobering, the expenditure of manpower staggering. They found a regimentation of mind, all their informants, whether educated or uneducated, repeating the clichés instilled by the regime.

The revolution of which the People's Republic of China is a stage and which has been developing since the 1890's is far from ended. When the next stage will come and what form it will take cannot be safely predicted.

The Republic of China since 1949

In 1949, when the Republic of China was forced off the mainland, its future was precarious. It has owed its continuation partly to the

Chinese who supported it and partly to the United States. It has made its headquarters on Taiwan (Formosa) and also holds possession of the Pescadores (Panghu) in the straits slightly west of Taiwan and of a few islands close to the mainland, chiefly Matsu and Quemoy, off the coast of Fukien. As on the mainland, the Republic of China is controlled by the Kuomintang. Chiang Kai-shek, the President, successively re-elected as his terms expired, has insisted that the Communist rule of the mainland is ephemeral, that the Republic of China is still the only legitimate regime, and that he will return to the mainland, defeat the Communists, and re-establish the full authority of the Republic of China. In the meantime, in principle the structure of the national government has been continued and Taiwan has been administered as one of the provinces of the Republic.

At the outset the support of the United States was not fully assured. During the Japanese invasion, and especially after Japan's attack on Pearl Harbor (December, 1941) which brought the United States into World War II, substanital aid had been given by the United States to the Republic of China. When the United States, after the defeat of Japan, sought to end the civil war by bringing the Kuomintang and the Communists together, each loudly accused the Americans of helping the other. Yet the United States gave support in funds and arms, not to the Communists, but to the Republic of China as the government which it recognized. After the Communist victory, for a time the United States maintained consular and diplomatic representation on the mainland, but Communist intransigence soon made that impossible and American personnel was brought home (January, 1950). In the United States powerful voices were raised in advocacy of continued aid to the Republic of China, although at first (January 5, 1950) President Truman said that his government would not accord military assistance to the Chiang Kai-shek regime.

However, when in June, 1950, war broke out in Korea, Truman ordered the American fleet to prevent any Communist attack on Taiwan or the Pescadores, but he asked the Republic of China and that government agreed to cease its air attacks on the mainland and to desist from its blockade of the coast.

The United States continued to assist the Republic of China through financial support and advisory personnel for the armed forces and the economic improvement of Taiwan. In February, 1953, when President Eisenhower said that the American Navy would no longer shield the Republic of China, Chiang Kai-shek assented, for he interpreted it as permission to invade the mainland. In 1955 the United States and the Republic of China signed a treaty for mutual defense against the attack of any enemy. Although several non-Communist countries, among them the United Kingdom, which, while continuing consular relations with the Republic of China, entered into diplomatic relations with the People's Republic of China, the United States was able to prevent the Communist regime from being admitted to the United Nations. Until 1962 the votes by which this was achieved were by a progressively narrowing margin. Then, as we have seen, Peking's actions on the Indian border aroused wide resentment and fear, and more votes were registered against admission.

The People's Republic of China was adamant in its purpose to "liberate" Taiwan, and from time to time its batteries shelled Matsu and Quemoy. In the spring and summer of 1962 the reports of internal difficulties on the mainland encouraged some in the Republic of China to believe that the time was opportune for an invasion to restore its authority in its former territories. To counter an attempt the People's Republic of China massed troops opposite Taiwan and resumed the bombardment of the offshore islands. The United States tactfully but pointedly told both belligerents that it would not support such an invasion.

The Record in Taiwan

On Taiwan the Republic of China faced major difficulties. Since 1895 the island had been ruled by the Japanese and in language and customs the Taiwanese had been partly assimilated. The vast majority of the Taiwanese were Chinese, for the aborigines were in mountain fastnesses and were small minorities. But for several generations the Taiwanese had lived on the island and had an exaggerated provincial particularism which had traditionally characterized the Chinese. For the most part the mainlanders who had taken refuge on the island used Mandarin. To the Taiwanese, whose language was that of the neighboring coastal provinces, Mandarin was unintelligible, and because of the Japanese educational system, the speech of their late masters was their second language. After the defeat of the Japanese and before the arrival of Chiang Kai-shek and his army, the governor first appointed by the Republic of China was corrupt, exploited the Taiwanese, and killed many of them. To the Taiwanese, therefore, the mainlanders were far worse than the Japanese had ever been. When they arrived, the mainlanders were torn by factions. Chiang Kai-shek maintained his power by severe methods. Moreover, he had to face the chronic menace of Communist infiltration. In addition, a large army—about 600,000 strong—was maintained to guard against invasion and to take advantage of opportunities to recapture the mainland. An increase in population added to the difficulties. The census showed 7,617,000 in 1950 and 9,874,450 in 1956, both totals including mainlanders who made up between a fifth and a fourth of the whole.

In spite of the adverse beginnings, by 1964 the Republic of China had registered encouraging progress on Taiwan. It had accomplished "land reform," not by the violent confiscation of land through which the Communists had achieved it on the mainland, but by the purchase of the holdings of the landlords and the distribution of them, together with government land, among the cultivators. It thus avoided the executions and the class bitterness which had attended the Communist agrarian measures. The Republic of China declared that by 1954 tenancy had been reduced to a fifth of the farm acreage. By 1964 rapid progress in industrialization was being achieved. The Republic of China stressed education, and as early as 1954 it was reported that nine-tenths of the children of school age were in elementary schools. Through the schools language uniformity was furthered by teaching the *kuo-yü*, the standardized form of the Mandarin which had been promoted by the Nationalists even before 1949. Schools for adults were also conducted. In 1954 it was claimed that illiteracy had been reduced from 35.6 per cent in 1949 to 17.76 per cent. Secondary and higher schools were also multiplied. As it had before 1949 on the mainland, the curriculum included the *Three Principles of the People* (*San Min Chu I*) through which Sun Yat-sen had set forth his program for the country. This emphasis was because the Kuomintang was still dominant and had Sun Yat-sen as its professed ideal. The curriculum included the Confucian Classics as well as modern Western subjects in an attempt to conserve the best of the Confucian heritage combined with what was deemed useful in Western civilization. Efforts were made to integrate the Taiwanese with the mainlanders in schools, in the use of the *kuo-yü*, and in universal military conscription. Taiwanese were accorded a major share of participation in the local governments and to a degree, as yet very limited, in the national structure. Much effort was expended on improving economic conditions: railways were put into working order, highways were constructed, new hydroelectric installations furnished additional power for industries, transportation, and lighting, and the food supply was augmented by improved agricultural methods. In contrast with the mainland, little serious undernourishment was seen. Public health measures were promoted. By 1964 rice production per acre was about as high as in Japan—higher than elsewhere in East Asia. Exports mounted, of both manufactures and foodstuffs. Because of the progress, the United States announced that in 1965 it would discontinue economic aid, as no longer needed. It would, however, continue assistance to defense. All this was an attempt to demonstrate that a non-Communist regime could accomplish more for a body of mankind in East Asia than could the communism which prevailed on the mainland of China.

Outwardly the mainlanders professed their purpose to return to their homes, and on this Chiang Kai-shek was adamant; yet in 1964 the more thoughtful were aware that the possibility of this step was increasingly remote. They had not shared in the experiences of those who since 1949 had been under the People's Republic of China and so, if they returned, they would be comparative strangers.

Transition

This was the situation in China in 1964, both on the mainland and Taiwan. The largest fairly homogeneous body of people on the globe, heirs of an ancient and highly developed civilization, were in the midst of a vast revolution, due primarily to the impact of the West. Change had begun to be apparent in the middle of the nineteenth century and had assumed major dimensions in the decades before and after 1900. In the 1950's and the early 1960's in the People's Republic of China the revolution has been at a stage in which communism has controlled the large majority of the Chinese. A minority in islands off the coast have been under a regime, the Republic of China, which represents a slightly earlier stage. With the future highly uncertain, all that the interested and informed observer can confidently predict is further change into another stage of the revolution. When that will come and what form or forms it could take he does not know. But he can be sure that it will be of major importance for the rest of mankind.

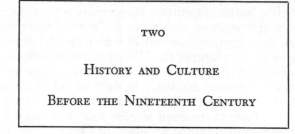

TWO

HISTORY AND CULTURE

BEFORE THE NINETEENTH CENTURY

Again and again in the preceding chapter the importance of the geographic setting and the pre-twentieth century history of the Chinese has been apparent. Out of that geography and that history came the China of the 1950's and 1960's, and the mentality and the policies of the Chinese of today.

In the main, the area with which we are concerned can be divided into what can be called China proper and the outlying dependencies. The distinction is partly racial and partly geographic. China proper has been occupied primarily by those whom we have called the Han Chinese. Its physical features have helped to shape the culture of the Chinese and have done much to determine the economy and policies of the regimes which have sought to govern China. In the outlying dependencies the Han Chinese are minorities, but they have aspired to be ruling minorities. Physiographically the outlying dependencies border on China proper and constitute natural frontiers. From time to time one or another of these border peoples have endeavored to master part or all of China proper. Some of them have succeeded, several of them for centuries, but none of them permanently. To defend China proper the major ruling houses of that area strove to bring the outlying regions under their control, and some of their conquests were permanently incorporated into China proper. Not until the eighteenth century with the Ch'ing or Manchu dynasty did any ruling line bring all of the outlying dependencies under one sway. As we have noted, both the governments which followed the

Ch'ing, those of the Republic of China and the People's Republic of China, claimed these areas as legitimately theirs.

The Geographic Setting

Through the centuries the area peopled by the Han Chinese has progressively expanded. In the second millennium B.C., it embraced the lower reaches of the valley of the Huangho and the adjacent highlands and mountains. By the dawn of the twentieth century it covered what were known as the Eighteen Provinces, the administrative device by which it was governed. In the twentieth century the Han Chinese pressed into Manchuria, from its name obviously the ancestral home of the Manchus. By the mid-twentieth century the Han Chinese were in the overwhelming majority and Manchuria was known by them as the Northeast, or the Northeastern Provinces. As the Han Chinese expanded they either assimilated the non-Chinese or administered them as non-assimilated minorities. The assimilation was partly by intermarriage and partly by acculturation. The Han Chinese had little race prejudice, but they displayed a profound conviction of cultural superiority. If a people conformed to their culture the Han Chinese were relatively tolerant of differences in blood. In the twentieth century something of that attitude has persisted. For example, in theory the Communists have permitted the non-Chinese to live according to their ancestral institutions. Practically, they have endeavored to bring them to the acceptance of socialism as interpreted by the Chinese Communist Party.

Nature fitted China proper to be the home of a great civilization not only in pre-twentieth century times but also in the age of industrialization. Even in the days before steamship, railways, automobiles, and airplanes, natural barriers to cultural unity, while formidable, were not insuperable. They were sufficiently marked to encourage provincial particularism and loyalties. But the institutions created by the Han Chinese were able to transcend them and to weld China proper into a cultural and usually into a political unity.

China proper has river systems which permitted a high degree of communication by the facilities available even before the mechanical devices imported from the West. Two major streams, the Yangtze and the Huangho, with their tributaries, drain most of the area. A third stream, smaller, the Hsi Kiang (West River), empties into an estuary on which the city of Canton arose. The Northeastern Provinces (Manchuria) also have rivers—the Sungari, Liao, and Yalu, the latter on the southeastern border. Most of the rivers are navigable and facilitate the unity of the country. That is especially true of the Yangtze and its tributaries. On one long stretch, the gorges through which the Yangtze finds its way through the mountains which separate the great western province of Szechuan from the river's lower valley, navigation is difficult, but through the centuries hardy and skillful boatmen have made them a major artery of domestic commerce and in modern times high-powered steamers have plied them. In the lower reaches ocean freighters have regularly come to Hankow, five hundred miles from the river's mouth. The Yellow River takes its name from the heavy load of sediment, largely of the yellow earth, the loess, which blankets much of its valley. In its upper reaches, because of its swift current, it is not as navigable as the Yangtze, and it is still less so on its lower course.

China proper possesses large areas of fertile soil. Most of them are in the valleys of the main rivers and their tributaries. Chief among them are alluvial plains built by the Yangtze, Yellow, and West rivers, and a basin in the western province of Szechuan, drained by the Min River, which empties into the Yangtze. Fertility is aided by the loess, composed of dust of wind-borne origin, in places sifted by streams. As population mounted, the industrious Chinese farmer terraced the hillsides. He also has made extensive use of irrigation and fertilizers with which long experience has made him familiar.

Yet the rivers which have created the alluvial plains have also been a source of disaster. From time to time unusually heavy rainfalls have given rise to floods which have submerged thousands of square miles and have contributed to famines that have cost millions of lives. The Huangho has often been called "China's sorrow." Because of its heavy load of silt it builds up its bed and natural dikes. Human effort sometimes helps build the dikes, but when the latter are neglected or in times of prolonged downpours, it breaks through these restrictions and spreads over the plain which is below the level of its bed. Across the centuries it has several times altered its mouth from north to south and from south to north of the Shantung promontory with tragic loss of life.

In general, the climate is favorable, since most of China proper is in the temperate zone. Only the extreme South is on the northern borders of the tropics. For the most part the rainfall is sufficient for agriculture. It is heaviest in the south along the coast, and declines with increasing distance from the southern seas which are its main source. But even in the north the clouds supply enough moisture directly to the soil and through the streams to make crops possible. The climate is monsoonal, so that even in the south, the north wind brings bracing autumns. In the North winters are cold and dry, and millet and wheat are the prevailing grains while in the Yangtze Valley and the south, rice is the chief cereal. In addition, the soy bean is an extensive source of protein and vegetable oil.

In several earlier periods the population of the Chinese Empire equaled or surpassed that of any contemporary realm—notably that of the Roman, Arab, and Turkish empires at their height. In the nineteenth century it was larger than the next most populous empire, that of Great Britain. In the eighteenth century the population had a phenomenal growth, and its striking increase in the twentieth century constituted a major problem.

China proper, if in it is included the North-eastern provinces, possesses natural resources ample for the industrial age of the twentieth century. Its deposits of coal are enormous. Indeed, coal had been used as fuel for several centuries before it was so employed in Western Europe. Iron is in abundant supply, and though petroleum is not as plentiful as coal and iron, by the 1960's quantities of oil shale have been revealed which, if economical methods of distillation can be developed, will remedy that deficiency. China's rivers could be harnessed to supply prodigious amounts of hydroelectric power. That is especially true of the Yangtze gorges and of the Huangho where, by an abrupt turn, it issues from the mountains onto the North China plain. Combined with the industry and intelligence of the Chinese, these resources gave promise of the enormous industrial development which the Communists hope will be one of their achievements.

The Outlying Dependencies

On the south, west, and north, China proper is bordered by areas of major importance in its past, its present, and for its future. At one time or another they have been brought within the domains of the rulers of China proper. Together they embrace far more square miles than does China proper. In the eighteenth and nineteenth centuries, when, under the Manchus, the Empire reached its widest extent, it embraced Tibet, Sinkiang, Inner Mongolia, Outer Mongolia, and Manchuria. In a political relationship which was a feature of the Chinese Empire of that day but which had no exact parallel in the Occident, Tongking, Burma, Nepal, and Korea were also in the category of dependencies, but were not directly governed by officials appointed from Peking, as were the others.

The outlying territories have several features which are important for an understanding of the history of China and particularly of the China of the twentieth century. As will be seen by a glance at the map, they extend the Chinese realms to its natural geographic boundaries. That has been true especially in Tibet and Nepal where the mighty Himalayas stand between India and the north. It has also been apparent in Sinkiang and Mongolia, where the mountainous backbone of Asia has constituted the western and northwestern barrier separating the Chinese Empire from Central Asia and Siberia.

The strongest rulers of China have considered that control of the outlying dependencies is essential to the peace of China proper, for from before the Christian era these regions have been the sources of invasions. They are arid or semiarid and their peoples have viewed with covetous eyes the fertile and well-watered valleys and plains of China proper. Repeatedly China proper has been conquered in part or in whole from these areas. Tongking and Burma have never been the sources of serious menace, Korea had been such only as a highway for Japanese armies, so the drive to bring these countries into the domains of the rulers of China proper arose primarily from imperialistic ambitions. But Tibet, Sinkiang, Mongolia, and Manchuria have again and again been the sources of invasions. Indeed, in the thirteenth and fourteenth centuries the Mongols and in the seventeenth, eighteenth, and nineteenth centuries the Manchus mastered all of China proper. To defend China proper its rulers have not only sought to master these regions but as well erected and long maintained the Great Wall.

Foreign merchants long frequented the ports on the south coast, but they did not attempt territorial conquests. In the sixteenth century Japanese pirates raided the coast, but they did not aspire to permanent footholds. Only in the second half of the nineteenth century and in the twentieth century did the ocean become a highway for conquest. China's territorial defenses had been on the northern land frontiers, and this was one of the reasons the Chinese were so easily overrun by Westerners and the Japanese, possessed as they were of command of the sea. Even the People's Republic of China has faced landward and, except for submarines and incipient air power, could not present an adequate defense from powers, the United States in particular, which has controlled the adjacent oceans.

Significantly, the Chinese have never fully incorporated in their

Empire areas beyond the natural barriers. The generals of two great dynasties, the Han and the T'ang, carried Chinese arms beyond them, but only for a few decades and then only in Central Asia where caravan routes connected China with the lands to the west.

In none of the outlying dependencies except Manchuria, and in that not until the twentieth century, have the Han Chinese constituted more than small minorities. They have come as soldiers, administrators, and merchants, but Tibet, Sinkiang, and Mongolia are climatically unfavorable to the agricultural economy of the Han Chinese. Inner Mongolia is a partial exception, but only because, being a region of marginal rainfall, in decades when the precipitation encouraged them, Han Chinese moved in and competed with the pastoral Mongols.

The outlying dependencies constituted a barrier which partially isolated the Han Chinese from other cultures and so bred in them the sense of cultural superiority which long characterized them and of which the Republic of China and especially the People's Republic of China have been heirs. But the isolation has been far from complete. From the earliest times contributions came from other peoples, the usual channels being the trade routes across Sinkiang and merchants on the south coast. But until the latter half of the nineteenth and the first six decades of the twentieth century, none of these influences bred what could be called a revolution. The nearest approach to exceptions have been Buddhism and Islam. But from the ninth century Buddhism has been a waning force and Moslems have never been more than minorities. Ultimately the Han Chinese assimilated what reached them from abroad and integrated it into their basic cultural patterns which prevailed into the twentieth century. The Republic of China, under Chiang Kai-shek, and more obviously, and basically and more insistently, the Communists have been convinced that Chinese culture as shaped by them is ideally the best for all mankind. More nearly isolated from the rest of the world than China had been since the last decade of the nineteenth century, the Communists are convinced that theirs is the true version of Marxist socialism and that by their achievements they will prove to the rest of mankind that theirs is the wave of the future.

The Historical Setting: The Beginnings

If we are to understand Chinese communism and its leaders, we must have some knowledge of the long history out of which they have come. Mao Tse-tung, Chou En-lai, Liu Shao-ch'i, Chu Tê, and their colleagues, as we have seen, are both rebels and patriots. They are rebels partly because they are patriots, for they see in the institutions and customs which they reject a major source of China's weakness before the aggressive Occident. They revolted against institutions and customs which they had known in their youth, partly because they were fierce nationalists, infected by the passion for nationhood, a passion which has been associated with Western civilization and which is flooding the earth in this century. But in their youth they had been exposed to the classical inheritance of China and were both consciously and unconsciously influenced by it. Just as Westerners, including Americans, are the heirs, usually half-consciously or unconsciously, of a civilization rooted in the Tigris-Euphrates and Nile valleys and are even more indebted to Palestine, Greece, Rome, Christianity, and later developments in Europe, and just as Russian Communists, self-conscious revolutionists, bear the impress of what has come to them from Byzantium and through Marx and Engels from Protestant Christianity and nineteenth century Western European socialism, so the Chinese Communists, notably those of the generation now in power, bear the imprint not only of what they have adopted from the West, but also, and fully as much, of all of China's past. They and those directed by them eagerly study that past, reinterpreting it through what they believe has been received from Marxism-Leninism. To that past we must now turn, stressing features which seem to have a bearing on the Chinese communism of the 1950's and 1960's.

The beginnings of Chinese civilization were in the Northeast of what eventually became China proper, and are still shrouded in obscurity. But in the past half century extensive light has been shed on them.

In recent decades remains of what seem to have been the earliest men in China have been discovered in caves near Peking. Hundreds of thousands of years old, a feature of their skeletons has been interpreted as showing them to have been among the ancestors of the present Chinese. Many centuries later, but before the winds deposited the loess over much of the north of China proper, came the paleolithic men whose hearths and stone implements have been found underneath that covering. They, too, were in North China, the home of the earliest Chinese civilization. Another shorter gap of centuries separated these Paleolithic men from the Late Stone Age or neolithic culture which clearly made contributions to the later China most obviously in the form of implements and pottery examples of which survived the years. The peoples who produced the pottery and the villages which have been excavated were clearly agricultural, and in that respect at least they were the predecessors of the later Han Chinese.

Sometime in the second millennium B.C. an agriculturally based state called Shang arose, also in North China on the alluvial plain in the lower reaches of the valley of the Yellow River. Cultural development from the Shang era to the China of the twentieth century is continuous. The Shang culture emerged later than those of the Nile Valley, the Tigris-Euphrates Valley, and possibly the Valley of the Indus, but how far, if at all, it was indebted to one or more of these cultures is not known. The Shang had a form of writing which was clearly indigenous. Archaeology has discovered what are almost certainly its earliest forms, which under the Shang were further developed to become rich and sophisticated. This written language was the ancestor of the written characters by which the Chinese have since written. Several capitals and written records of the Shang which have been unearthed and preserved disclose a civilization which contributed much to later centuries. The society was aristocratic, with class lines sharply drawn between the ruling minority and the underprivileged majority. The society was warlike, and the rank and file made this possible by their toil in the fields. Grains, such as millet, still cultivated, provided much of the food; domestic animals abounded, among them pigs, sheep, dogs, and fowls—again a continuing characteristic of China. The foundations of buildings which have been uncovered show that the architecture was the prototype of that developed in later centuries. Religion was a prominent feature of the culture, with sacrifices to rivers and the earth and ceremonies in honor of ancestors and various divinities. The chief god was Shang Ti. Much of the Shang religion, modified (the two Shangs of the dynasty and the religion are written as different characters), was continued into the twentieth century and was displaced only by the irruption of the West. No priestly class existed, but experts directed the ceremonies, both religious and secular, and they are said to have been the precursors of the scholar class which set the standards in later China.

In the twelfth century B.C., the Shang were conquered by the Chou. Racially the Chou seem to have been related to the Shang and culturally they may have had much in common. However, the Chou were a ruder people. Their territorial center was farther west, in the valley of the Wei, a tributary of the Huangho which debouches into that stream as the latter makes a sharp turn to the east to build up its alluvial plain. The Wei has a fertile valley in which the Chou had their first capital and which was to be the seat of the capitals of several later ruling lines.

For about nine centuries the Chou ruled the Chinese. Like the Shang, their monarchs bore the title of *wang* (king) who in the earlier centuries gave able leadership. Eventually, however, their functions became almost entirely ceremonial. Through them the tradition was nourished that all the Chinese should be embraced in a single, although locally varied, state. Here, too, a tradition existed which was to be so firmly engrained in the Chinese mind that both the Republic of China and the People's Republic of China held to it as axiomatic.

During the long centuries of the Chou the area embraced by Chinese civilization was greatly expanded. Before the third century B.C. it embraced not only the alluvial plain of the Huangho, as had the Shang, but also the valley of the Wei, mountainous regions to the north of the plain and the valley, much of the alluvial plain on the lower reaches of the Yangtze and its tributaries, the fertile valley off the upper Yangtze that constitutes the heart of the province of Szechuan, and the mountains which separate the mid-Yangtze from the Wei and part of the Huangho. As the area grew it became divided politically into many states, some large and some small. What has sometimes been known as feudalism existed, with local princes owing homage, tribute, and military service to the Chou *wang*, and lesser magnates under similar obligations to major lords. Although not precisely comparable to the European system which bore that designation, the system could be cited by the Communists as a confirmation of their interpretation of the history of China which included feudalism as a stage of development through which the country must pass in its progress toward socialism.

About the middle of the fifth century B.C., this "feudalism" began to wane. The period is known as that of the Contending, or Warring, States, during which the chief belligerents were mostly large principalities on the frontiers of the expanding China. The inhabitants were partly non-Chinese, but more and more they were assimilated to the Chinese cultural tradition. The Chou *wang* were progressively powerless figureheads and their rule was effective only over a diminishing area around their traditional capital. The sovereigns of some of the major states assumed the title of *wang*, thereby asserting their equality with the Chou. However, the dream of a realm united under one reigning house and with a common culture did not die but persisted to the days of the Republic of China and the People's Republic of China.

The Shaping of Chinese Culture

In the latter half of the period of Chou, the dream of unity was strengthened and given continuing form through intellectual activity which in its variety, originality, and intensity was not to be equaled in all the history of China. In free discussion the more thoughtful wrestled with the problems common to all men—the nature of man, the meaning, if any, of the natural environment in which man finds himself, and the ideas which should govern man as he seeks to create a society to meet his needs. Among the results were a frame of mind and a tradition which, with modifications, were to persist through the centuries and which were to underlie the governing attitudes of both the Republic of China and the People's Republic of China.

The intellectual ferment had many sharply contending aspects, but with all its variety certain common features emerged over the centuries which increasingly characterized the life and thought of China and which helped to shape the China of the 1950's and 1960's. (1) All China must be included in one political structure. For a time that unity might be lost, but it must and would be regained. (2) That unity, although political, could be effective only if based upon a common culture. (3) That culture must have at its foundation a single set of ideas, a controlling ideology. (4) That ideology must accord with the pattern of the universe and of human history; thus validity depends upon a correct understanding of the nature of the universe and of man, and of the manner in which this has been displayed in history. (5) Practically, this understanding will express itself in human society, society which must be the goal of thought and of action. That society will seek the collective welfare of all who are embraced in it. (6) Essential to that society is conformity by its members to ethical standards. (7) These ethical standards must have as their primary goal not the individual but society. Presumably through society the individual will find satisfaction and fullness of life, but these are secondary and the individual must subordinate his personal interests to society as a whole. (8) This ideology is to be inculcated by individuals who are educated in it, who are committed to it, and who are to have the leadership in the nation. (9) The culture realized in this fashion is the ideal and the norm for all mankind. Those who do not conform to it are "barbarians," who for their own good will be brought to accept it by the example of the obvious superiority of that culture.

As will be seen from this summary, whether consciously or unconsciously, in all points the People's Republic of China was heir to this tradition. The ideology by which it sought to bring China out of the weakness of the preceding decades was not indigenous, but it was modified to meet what Mao Tse-tung, Liu Shao-ch'i, and their associates conceived to be the concrete situation. In this they were following the precedent of Lenin in interpreting Marxism to take account of changing conditions. They were committed to Marxism-Leninism, not simply to Marx. They insisted that all China must be included in one political structure; that this unity must be based upon a common culture; that this culture must embody a single ideology; that Marxism-Leninism gives the correct understanding of the nature of the universe, of man, and of history; that this ideology will give rise to a particular kind of society; that this society will seek the collective welfare of all men, not only the Han Chinese but also the non-Han Chinese in the territories of the People's Republic of China, and, ultimately, of the inhabitants of all the globe; that this society must incorporate certain ethical ideals; that bringing all the Han Chinese to the convinced acceptance of the ideology is essential; and that the acceptance must be the responsibility of an elite, the members of the Communist Party, who are intelligently committed to Marxism-Leninism as interpreted by Mao Tse-tung and in their lives and actions are single-minded exemplars of that form of socialism.

The main schools of thought which emerged in the later centuries of the Chou were called Confucianism, Taoism, and Legalism.

Confucianism had as its chief figure Confucius who traditionally is thought to have lived between 551 and 479 B.C. He was born in one of the smaller states of the Chou era, now in Shantung province, and from his early years was an earnest student of China's past and of the literature which had been transmitted from antiquity. He regarded himself as a transmitter and interpreter of that past, and not a creator, and he idealized the past and saw in some of its rulers—now believed to have been largely mythical but accepted by him as historical—models for the princes of his day. He had the mind of a social philosopher who dreamed of a realm which would embrace all Chinese—indeed, all civilized men, for so he regarded the Chinese. His interest was an ideal human society, and for a model of that society he looked to the past—to the example of great rulers of antiquity who were believed to have been the creators of the Chinese state and to be the standard for succeeding rulers. He made much of the maintenance of traditional ceremonies as a means of producing good moral character in rulers and ruled and taught that the ideal society is to be achieved not by force but by the example of the monarchs and the upper classes. He stressed especially the cultivation of high character by scholars who would discipline themselves in morals and the observance of the customary ritual, and he emphasized the importance of the family. He was somewhat of an agnostic but had confidence in a ruling Power which makes for order and righteousness, and he performed the traditional religious observances as though the spirits which they were supposed to honor were present, but he declined to discuss the problem of a life after death. High-minded, courteous, a reverent student of what had come from the past with a conscientiousness which demanded daily self-examination, Confucius was more and more revered during succeeding centuries as the authoritative teacher and standard of the Chinese.

The Chinese Communists rejected Confucianism, but consciously or unconsciously conformed to some of its tenets. They dissented from the kind of family loyalty which it enjoined and would not look back to the model rulers whom Confucius had praised. They had no use for his respect for the traditional ceremonies. But, while not agreeing with him as to what the ideal should be, they had as their objective an ideal human society. They held, with him, that a perfect society could be attained under the leadership of men who were committed to the ideal and exemplified it and they made much of self-examination as a way of approaching the ideal.

Second only to Confucius in shaping Confucianism was Mencius, traditionally thought to have lived from 373 to 288 B.C. A native of the same state as Confucius, he also sought an ideal human society, but more than Confucius, he stressed the physical welfare of the masses as a feature of the ideal society. He denounced princes who did not make that their objective and he could be interpreted as justifying rebellion against unworthy rulers.

Hsün Tzǔ, or Hsün K'uang, the third outstanding shaper of Confucianism in the Chou period, was about thirty years younger than Mencius and lived at a time when strife between the contending states was mounting. Unlike Confucius and Mencius, he regarded the universe, including mankind, as governed by unvarying law and denied the existence of spiritual beings. Like his two predecessors, he sought the achievement of an ideal society but unlike Mencius, who regarded human beings as basically good and so as responsive to the worthy example of rulers and teachers, he held human nature to be fundamentally bad but improvable. He maintained that improvement could be made through education which should include the regular observance of the traditional ritual, the observance of customs inherited from the past, the example of princes, and the formulation and enforcement of laws. He opposed war and held that peace could be achieved and maintained by the effect of the obviously noble character of a prince on the people of a hostile state. He believed that the desire for a better standard of living—for food and clothing—was at the basis of much of the tension between states, and therefore he would have had princes seek to lessen the tension by improving the economic condition of their subjects. He stressed government as a means of obtaining these objectives.

A school of thought which arose in the Chou era, in direct opposition to Confucianism, was Taoism. Its classic formulation was in the Tao Tê Ching, which was generally believed to have been written by Lao Tzŭ, supposedly an older contemporary of Confucius. However, scholars now think that the Tao Tê Ching was probably of much later composition and that Lao Tzŭ may never have lived. The early Taoists reacted against all efforts to achieve an ideal society. They insisted that the way of the universe is inaction. The Tao Tê Ching taught that the Tao, the governing principle in the universe, cannot be fully known, but that it is against human striving for high character and for an ordered society. Taoists believed that the ideal society is one in which the people of one village dwell so near to another village that they can hear the cocks of that village crowing, but have no desire to establish contacts with it. Here was the absolute minimum of government and so the precise opposite of Communist practice, but here was a concern for an ideal human society closely coordinated with a conviction about the nature of the universe. Out of primitive Taoism emerged a religion which persisted, but as a waning force, into the twentieth century.

The school with which the Communists might be more nearly in agreement than with any others of the Chou period is that of the Legalists. As did most of the other schools and as do the Communists, the Legalists sought to end the internal disorder of their day and to achieve an ideal society in which all Chinese would profit. Unlike Confucius and Mencius, they did not trust to the moral example of rulers and the elite for the attainment of this end. They sought to achieve their purpose through a system of laws impartially and firmly administered. As the Communists were to do, they advocated the adaptation of the laws from time to time to changing circumstances. Some Legalists, as the Communists were to do, sought to have all capital owned by, and all commerce conducted by, the state. They would thus control prices and prevent inequalities in the ownership of property.

The Unification of China

The disorder and prolonged civil strife of the later centuries of the Chou were ended by the unification of all the area over which the Chinese and their culture had spread. That achievement came under the Ch'in, one of the controlling states. As was true of the Chou, Ch'in had its original seat in the Wei Valley. There its rulers adopted the principles and program of the Legalists, and when, in the last quarter of the third century before Christ, Ch'in subdued all its rivals and ended the last ephemeral shadow of Chou power, its rulers, as the Communists were later to do, sought to create a new China. Although the Chou are traditionally called the third dynasty of China, the Shang being the second, and a Hsia about which little is known the first, the Ch'in statesmen really began the Chinese Empire. Fittingly, the name China is derived from the Ch'in, and the Ch'in ruler under whom China was united assumed a new title, Shih Huang Ti, usually translated the First Emperor.

At the outset Shih Huang Ti's domains embraced most of the valley of the Huangho, the highlands north of the Huangho, and the valleys of the Yangtze and its tributaries. This was the area over which Chinese culture had spread by the end of the Chou. In addition, Shih Huang Ti extended his rule along the coast south of the Yangtze into the later Tongking. His capital was in the valley of the Wei.

Several features of the regime of Shih Huang Ti established a pattern which was followed by Emperors in later centuries and which the People's Republic of China followed to an extent. Shih Huang Ti sought to unite all China under a single rule, and under him the dream of an inclusive political structure cherished by such men as Confucius, Mencius, and Hsün Tzŭ became a reality. Even though for periods, some of them long, China was again divided, the ideal persisted, and the times of disunion progressively became shorter. In seeking to bring all China proper within the People's Republic of China and to extend its borders, the Communists were conforming to a tradition which had been made effective by the Ch'in dynasty and which had precedent under the Chou and even the Shang. To accomplish his purpose of unifying China, Shih Huang Ti adopted a number of measures, several of which were duplicated by the Communists—although not necessarily with conscious imitation. Shih Huang Ti sought to enforce compliance with the program of one of the schools of thought inherited from the Chou, that of the Legalists, and he endeavored to suppress all the other schools. Except for copies preserved in the imperial library, the writings of the rivals of the Legalists were ordered destroyed and discussions and debates between the adherents of the various schools which had enlivened the later centuries of the Chou were forbidden. New and simpler forms of the historic characters were devised and made uniform for the realm, roads centering in the capital were constructed to facilitate communication throughout the Empire, vast public works were constructed, by a lavish expenditure of forced labor, including canals and a wall along the northern frontiers to facilitate defense against the non-Chinese who were seeking to press into the fertile valleys of China proper. Through compulsory movements of populations newly conquered territories were incorporated into the Empire.

The regime established by Shih Huang Ti and the great ministers who served under him did not long survive its creators, for the empire was restive under the restrictions of the Ch'in and after the death of Shih Huang Ti no one emerged who was able to curb the unrest. Within the decade which followed the demise of the First Emperor the Ch'in dynasty collapsed.

In the civil strife which accompanied and followed the fall of the Ch'in, a warrior emerged who founded the Han dynasty which, except for an interruption of fifteen years early in the first century B.C., persisted from 206 B.C. to A.D. 220. The founder of the Han was not, as Shih Huang Ti had been, from the nobility of the Chou era; in the rough and tumble of civil strife he emerged from the masses.

By a development which began with its first Emperor, under the

Han dynasty an ideological basis was created for the Chinese state which, with modifications, persisted to the opening years of the twentieth century. That basis was a combination of Confucianism and Legalism in which Confucianism predominated. In principle and largely in fact the government was still autocratic. However, administration was increasingly by officials who were trained in Confucian ideals. To prevent the Empire from disintegrating into a loose collection of principalities under hereditary rulers, as had been the experience in the Chou era, the Han sought to recruit officials on the basis of worth rather than birth. To discover administrators of ability and integrity the Han depended partly on the recommendations of men whom its Emperors trusted, but the Han also inaugurated the beginnings of civil service examinations which were to be elaborated by later dynasties. The examinations were based chiefly on books which Confucian scholars deemed authoritative summaries of the teachings of their school and which embodied a description of the history and institutions of China as understood by that school and the literature which it prized. The effect of this system was the emergence of a bureaucracy committed to a particular ideology and because of the prestige of the governing officialdom, that ideology gradually became accepted for all Chinese of whatever social rank. Thus a unity was given to Chinese culture which persisted through the centuries. Though dynasties disintegrated and the Empire was sometimes divided and even ruled by aliens, cultural unity continued and helped to make possible political unity.

The Confucianism which undergirded this unity was not unchanging; in fact, the modifications which it displayed were often striking and, indeed, were indications of its vitality. Yet it continued to revere Confucius as its chief creator and exponent and in time shrines were erected in which he, his chief disciples, and his outstanding interpreters were officially honored by the state and by the scholar-officials trained in the classics revered by the Confucian school.

Here was a precedent to which, presumably without conscious intent, the Republic of China and the People's Republic of China were conforming. Each sought to promote the integration of China by achieving a cultural unity based on the intensive propagation of a set of convictions. In this in 1964 the Communists were more successful than the Nationalists.

The Han dynasty had other achievements which give it a distinct and important place in the history of China. Prominent among them were its conquests. In the decades which followed the collapse of the Ch'in dynasty, much of the south coast resumed the independence which Shih Huang Ti had attempted to erase. In the second and first centuries B.C. not only was Chinese rule re-established in that region, but it was extended as well into portions of the Southeast which had not submitted to the Ch'in, and the populations there gradually became Chinese in culture. In the Northeast the Han conquered much of what was later Southern Manchuria and Northern Korea and moved Chinese settlers into the area to hold it to the Empire. One result was the partial assimilation of that area to Chinese culture. Chinese arms were carried across what was later Sinkiang and, fleetingly, into what are now the southeastern portions of the U.S.S.R.

The Han dynasty was roughly contemporary with the earlier years of the Roman Empire, and some indirect commerce by sea existed with the Mediterranean world. Still indirect but more extensive was the exchange of goods via the deserts and oases of what we now know as Sinkiang. The chief export from China was silk, while imports included glass, jade, horses, ivory, precious stones, and fine cloths of wool and linen.

The conquests are evidence that the Chinese cherished imperialistic ambitions which persisted and were pursued under each of the major dynasties. In seeking to establish their rule over all the area which had ever acknowledged the sovereignty or even the tenuous suzerainty of a Chinese Emperor and in extending their influence over Chinese in Southeast Asia, both the Republic of China and the People's Republic of China have conformed to a time-honored precedent.

The Han dynasty was notable for striking cultural developments. In art it witnessed major contributions; philosophic discussions were not as uninhibited and creative as under the later centuries of the Chou, but they revived; some independent thinkers appeared; Confucianism flourished and was modified. The remnants of the literature banned by the Ch'in and decimated by the civil strife which accompanied and followed the demise of that dynasty were diligently sought and, when regained, were edited. New literature was written and a new prose style was developed and great histories were compiled: the most famous, that by Ssŭ-ma Ch'ien (145-? 87 B.C.), set a standard for a succession of later histories. Long before the Han, as we have suggested, the Chinese were historically minded; then and in subsequent centuries they created a more extensive body of historical literature than has any other people before the nineteenth and twentieth centuries, and although the Communists have insisted on rewriting it to make it conform to their convictions, in stressing history they have been true to a well-established Chinese tradition.

Under the Han, as under the Ch'in and, latterly, by the Communists, great public works were put through: canals were dug, and a dangerous flood of the Huangho was curbed; irrigation was emphasized; a highway was constructed to tie the North to the South and the Southwest. A state monopoly of salt and iron was created. By buying grain when it was plentiful and selling it in times of scarcity the state made a profit and reduced fluctuations in the price level.

The territorial expansion and the commerce under the Han dynasty brought China into touch with other cultures, and as a result many contributions came from abroad. Foreign influences on Chinese civilization were not a novelty; they had been entering for hundreds of years. Some were by way of the South but more through the long desert routes across what is now Sinkiang.

Of all the contributions from abroad, most profound and widespread in its effects was Buddhism. The Buddha who founded that religion was roughly a contemporary of Confucius. In the centuries which had elapsed between his death and the Han dynasty the faith which looked to him as its pathfinder had spread over much of India and had reached into the present Afghanistan—from which roads led to the Han domains—and Buddhism had developed distinctive philosophies and artistic forms. Precisely when and by what channels —whether by sea or the overland route—it first reached China we do not know, but it is clear that before the end of the second century A.D. communities of Buddhist monks were in existence in more than one part of China. However, the great growth of Buddhism in China came not during the Han, but later.

Under the Han China was one of the great empires of the day. In land area and in population it probably approximated the dimensions of the realm which was built by Rome. In the richness and variety of its culture the Han Empire ranked with the Mediterranean world and the India of its day. Appropriately, the Chinese looked back to the Han centuries as a great era and called themselves *Han jen*, "the men of Han." Hence we have spoken of those committed to Chinese culture as the Han Chinese. As did the Roman Empire the Han Empire showed great extremes of wealth and poverty; the court knew scenes of luxury, but the wars brought impoverishment to the masses.

Toward the close of the second century A.D. disorder increased.

Confucian theory had centered the state in the Emperor, and the imperial line declined and a succession of weak puppets were placed on the throne by rival factions. Floods, droughts, and domestic wars brought wide famine, thousands of peasants were poverty-stricken, many turned to banditry, other thousands wandered about, displaced persons, who were willing listeners to any who promised a better day. Revolts broke out, some of them led by bands called the Yellow Turbans who had espoused a form of Taoism. In A.D. 220 the Han, now feeble, came to an inglorious end.

A Period of Disunion

Following the collapse of the Han came more than three-and-a-half centuries of disunion. But the dream of a united China did not disappear: various ambitious warriors aspired to master all the area which had been ruled by the Han and to found dynasties which would renew the Empire. As time passed an uneasy division was seen between the Yangtze Valley, where rulers of Chinese blood and culture set up states, and the North, where non-Chinese invaders from the Northwest and the Northeast mastered the fertile plains and valleys inhabited by the Han Chinese. The barriers erected by Shih Huang Ti were breached.

During the centuries of internal weakness and division Chinese culture was more modified by contact with alien peoples and chiefly with Buddhism than it was to be until late in the nineteenth and in the twentieth century. The spread of the foreign faith was due partly to the disappearance of the monolithic political structure created by the Ch'in and by the Han Confucianism. The native culture could not offer the resistance to an alien religion which it had presented under these two strong dynasties. At the same time Buddhism was propagated by zealous missionaries and by Chinese converts. It was then prospering in India, Ceylon, and in several regions in Southeast Asia, and was at the height of its religious and cultural activity. Some missionaries came by the sea through ports on the south coast and others arrived overland by way of the Northwest. Zealous Chinese journeyed to India to drink of the heady stream at its source and brought back quantities of the literature that had been created in that land, much of which was translated into Chinese. With Buddhism came new forms of architecture, painting, images, and sculpture; Chinese religion and Chinese thought were profoundly modified; consciously or unconsciously, Taoism borrowed much from the foreign faith and Buddhist deities and Buddhist ideas were incorporated in folk religion and ethics. In the course of the centuries, then and later, the religion of the vast majority of the Chinese, both the masses and the intelligentsia, became a syncretic combination of Confucianism, Taoism, Buddhism, and of beliefs and practices which could be traced to none of the three major faiths.

During the long centuries of disunion, recurring civil strife, and foreign invasion, Chinese culture did not mark time. It was not suffering from the decline which was contemporaneously in progress in the Mediterranean world. An extensive movement of Han Chinese to the Yangtze Valley was seen and for the first time that region became a significant center of Chinese culture, partially assimilating non-Chinese elements in the area. The immigrants accommodated themselves to the climate and soil of the area, and wet cultivation of rice became common. Tea drinking arose as a custom in the Yangtze Valley and farther south: several centuries elapsed before it spread to the North. During intervals and in areas of comparative peace literature flourished and extensive libraries were collected. Such mechanical devices as the wheelbarrow and the water mill made their appearance, and for the first time we hear of coal as a fuel. In the North many among the non-Chinese invaders conformed to Chinese culture.

Commerce continued and with it went cultural contacts with other peoples. Contributions from abroad included the introduction of the cultivated walnut, the pomegranate, new methods of manufacturing glass, and forms of brocades. China was also contributing to other peoples. Chinese culture was a strong influence in Korea and began also markedly to influence Japan. The Japanese adopted Chinese characters although the Japanese language, previously without written form, was basically different from Chinese. To write it by means of Chinese characters was as much a *tour de force* as it would have been to give English a literary form by that means, yet eventually that was the medium employed by the Japanese. With Chinese characters came Chinese literature and extensive modifications in spoken Japanese. Chinese immigrants came to Japan and with them some industries were introduced.

New Power and Cultural Brilliance

Near the close of the sixth century A.D. the dream of embracing all China under one imperial rule again became a reality, first under the short-lived Sui dynasty (A.D. 589-618), and then for nearly three centuries (A.D. 618-907) under the T'ang dynasty.

Although the Sui held dominion for only a little over twenty-five years, its achievements were noteworthy. Its founder, a successful general (as, indeed, were the founders of all dynasties), began the construction of a new capital. It was in the Wei Valley, where the Ch'in and the early Han had had their capitals and was given the name Ch'ang-an, which had been that of the city in which Han rule had first centered. But while near the Ch'ang-an of the Han, it was not on the same site. The first Sui Emperor had it deliberately laid out in rectangular streets and walls and of magnificent dimensions, and constructed canals to connect Ch'ang-an with the South and thus to transport to his capital supplies of food from that prosperous region. He developed an examination system for the recruitment of able officials and made it more elaborate than the one created by the Han. The second Sui Emperor was of abounding energy and arrogant ambition. He enlarged the canal system which had been one of his father's achievements, and further elaborated the civil service examinations. In contrast with his father, who, partly at the instance of a masterful empress, was a devout Buddhist, he emphasized Confucianism. He continued his father's vigorous foreign policy and sent expeditions into what are now Vietnam and Sinkiang. Several immense palaces were built and walls along the northern frontier were extended during his reign, constructed by levies of forced labor. That was not a novel practice and was to be repeated by later rulers and by the Communists. The second Emperor of the Sui pushed his realm beyond its resources and failed in an effort to conquer what we now know as South Manchuria and North Korea. This failure added to the unrest provoked by other measures resulted in revolt, and he was killed.

Under the T'ang, established by one of the rebels against the Sui, China reached an apex of power and wealth which in the earlier years of the dynasty made it the mightiest state in the world of its day. Only in later decades, when the T'ang had begun to wane, was China equaled by the empire which, under the impulse of the first flush of Islam, the Arabs were building in Western Asia, North Africa, and the Iberian Peninsula.

The T'ang continued and augmented several of the policies inaugurated by the Sui. It retained the Sui capital, Ch'ang-an, which became the largest city of the world, with a population of between two and three millions. On it converged merchants from Central and Western Asia who made it markedly cosmopolitan. The civil service examinations were elaborated. Although Taoism and Buddhism were honored at the court, Confucianism was further revived to the extent that in the state schools which were multiplied, veneration of Confucius was decreed. In each of the administrative units through which the realm was governed, a temple was erected to Confucius and in it not only the sage, but, as well, twenty-two famous scholars of that school, most of them of the Han, were given official recognition. Foreign conquests were resumed, with Chinese armies penetrating to what are now the southeastern regions of the U.S.S.R. and there coming into conflict with the expanding Arab power. Korea was eventually subdued. The Japanese who visited China in large numbers were so impressed with Ch'ang-an that they modeled their own capitals on it, first at Nara and then at what we now know as Kyoto. Confucianism achieved popularity in learned circles in Japan. Japanese Buddhist monks went to the shrines of their faith in China and on their return reinforced the Buddhism which was rapidly gaining ground. Chinese administrative patterns profoundly influenced the organization of the Japanese state.

Under the T'ang Chinese culture had a fresh flowering. Some of the greatest painting in all China's history was done and poetry was written which the Chinese of subsequent centuries esteemed as notable as any ever composed. The first examples of printing, still rather crude, are from T'ang times.

During the T'ang Buddhism reached the apex of its popularity in China, although attempts to curb Buddhism were made by the Emperors, notably one in A.D. 835 which sought to prevent the ordination of additional Buddhist monks and another in A.D. 846 which led to the confiscation of thousands of acres of monastery lands, the destruction of more than forty thousand Buddhist temples, and the return to secular life of more than a quarter of a million Buddhist monks and nuns. The strictures on Buddhism were due in part to the revival of Confucianism. The revival was encouraged by the development of the civil service examinations, for they were based partly, although not entirely, on the Confucian classics.

A major transition in Chinese history began in 755, induced by a rebellion in that year. Although the revolt was suppressed, it led to the abdication of the Emperor during whose reign T'ang culture had reached its apex. Contributory to the transition were economic factors emerging from the migrations from the North to the Yangtze Valley which had been in progress for several generations and changes in the land and tax structures. Another factor was the emergence of new official families from the civil service examinations and the concurrent decline of an older landed aristocracy. The mounting stress on Confucianism was also a cause and a symptom of change.

A Brief Renewal of Division

Although a partial recovery was achieved from the rebellion of the middle of the eighth century and in spite of the fact that the T'ang dynasty continued for about a century and a half, progressive weakness was the unhappy record. At court luxury and intrigues for power meant decay at the very keystone of the imperial structure. Outwardly the Empire was still imposing. But additional revolts broke out, and from the non-Chinese peoples who were chronically eying with longing the prosperous and fertile valleys to the east and south came invaders who broke through the imperial defenses.

The final collapse of the T'ang was in A.D. 907. Approximately a half century of division followed. But in spite of the disorder, cultural progress continued: the printing by wooden blocks invented under the T'ang was further developed and gave an impulse to literature and scholarship, a revised edition of the Confucian Classics was prepared and printed, painting was continued and issued in the remarkable advances of the next period.

Following the fall of the T'ang, however, until the twentieth century only for a little over two and a half centuries was all China again ruled by Han Chinese. Even during that interval the Empire did not extend far beyond China proper, and it was only under emperors of alien blood that imperial ambitions were again successfully pursued. With the exception of those two and a half centuries, in parts or all of China proper the governing houses were alien conquerors, and though China grew in population and wealth, that growth was under foreign direction.

The Sung Dynasty

For a time, in the latter part of the tenth century, a general of long Chinese ancestry succeeded in uniting the country and founding in A.D. 906 a new dynasty. That dynasty, the Sung, with varying fortunes, continued for slightly over three centuries. However, neither he nor his descendants were able to extend their rule over all

of China proper. Before many decades the Sung were confronted by
alien powers which tore away the North and then, in the second half
of the thirteenth century, subdued the South. First a Manchurian
people appeared on the scene, established a dynasty which they called
Chin (meaning Gold), captured the Sung monarch in his capital,
and carried him into exile. Another of the Sung imperial family
moved his capital from place to place and eventually fixed it in the
city now known as Hangchow, a site slightly south of the Yangtze,
near the sea, and in a picturesque setting of river, lake, and mountains. Intermittent war was waged between the Chin and the Sung.
The Chin established their capital at Yenching, approximately on
the site of the present Peking, and controlled most of the North.
They failed to win a continuing foothold south of the Yangtze, but
the Sung Emperors paid tribute to them.

In the second half of the twelfth century a new power, the Mongols, arose and in the following century conquered both the Chin
and the Sung. The military genius who wielded them into an effective fighting force was Temuchin, better known by the title Genghiz
Khan, "the Universal Emperor," accorded him by his people. The
son of a chief of one of the many Mongol tribes, he first brought
all Mongolia under his rule and then part of what is now Sinkiang.
He attacked the Chin, captured Yenching, and reduced the territory
of the Chin to a fragment south of the Huangho. He next directed
his energies to the west. There he captured the rest of Sinkiang and
carried his arms to the banks of the Indus, into Persia, and into
southeastern Europe. Genghiz Khan died before he could give the
coup de grâce to the Sung. However, he had created such a war ma-
chine that his descendants were able to bring to realization his dream
of mastering China. In A.D. 1234 they eliminated the Chin, completed
the reduction of Korea which had been begun by Genghiz Khan, and
in the west they captured Baghdad. They conquered a kingdom in
the southwest of what is now China proper and penetrated into
Tongking and then into south and central portions of China proper.
The able Kublai Khan, a grandson of Genghiz Khan, pressed the
prolonged campaign against the Sung who offered stubborn resistance, but were forced southward, until in A.D. 1279 their commanding general, taking the young Emperor in his arms, threw himself into
the sea off the coast of Kwangtung. From his capital at Cambaluc
(Khanbalik), the present Peking, Kublai ruled all China and was
accepted by the Mongols who governed the wide domains in Central

and Western Asia and in Southeastern Europe. For the first time in its history all China was under a foreign conqueror.

In spite of the political weakness of the Sung, under it China had one of its greatest periods of economic prosperity and cultural achievement. The center of the Empire was in the Yangtze Valley rather than in the valley of the Huangho. Many Chinese moved there from the North to escape the alien rulers. Great cities multiplied. Formerly the main urban centers had arisen as political capitals and prospered because they were the seat of the imperial administration. Some cities, among them Hangchow, still owed much of their prominence and wealth to that fact, yet increasingly cities arose from industry and trade. Under the Sung, Hangchow had more than a million inhabitants and owed its affluence both to the presence of the imperial court and the officialdom which gathered there and to extensive commerce by land, canals, and the sea. With the growth of urban life went greater specialization in crops and industry, farmers became less self-sufficient, domestic trade increased, money was more important, and means were devised for the transfer of funds from one part of the country to another.

The cultural creativity of the Sung was seen partly in political and social theory and its application to the policies of the state. The most influential and controversial figure was Wang An-shih, of the early and most vigorous years of the Sung who advocated the thorough reorganization of fiscal and military procedures, probably designed to improve the economic lot of the masses and to strengthen the Sung in its resistance to the northern invaders. Among the measures which he proposed were a budget for the state with an eye to large reductions in the cost of government; a state monopoly of commerce, with the produce of each district being applied first to the payment of taxes and the local needs and the surplus purchased by the state as a means of equalizing the supply between times of plenty and of dearth and as between the several parts of the Empire; state loans to farmers in the planting season to be repaid as crops were harvested; the abolition of the conscription of labor; changes in taxation, among them levies on all property, both real estate and movable, and in proportion to the wealth of the individual; compulsory military service; an improved system for obtaining horses for the cavalry needed for defense against the northern invaders; and a change in emphasis in the examinations through which officials were recruited—from literary style to the application of the classics to current problems. Some of these proposals bore heavily on the wealthy and gave rise to intense controversy. For a time the Emperor supported Wang An-shih, but later the program was alternatively adopted and rejected, and eventually most of it was abandoned. However, a portion became a continuing feature of imperial administration. Toward the end of the Sung a movement for land reform arose, but it, too, failed because of the opposition of the landlords.

The Sung period was also marked by intellectual activity stimulated by the preparation for the civil service examinations, for the Sung placed even more emphasis on these examinations than had the Han and the T'ang. A mounting proportion of officials were recruited through them, many from the Southeast where urbanization was most developed and numbers from social strata which were newly emerging, rather than from the North where the older standards of scholarship were maintained. The new men were, accordingly, less bound by tradition than were the Northerners. The intellectual ferment gave rise to debates which profoundly stirred scholarly circles. The controversy provoked by Wang An-shih was the leading political ingredient of the ferment while other aspects were more concerned with abstract philosophy. Out of the discussions came what is known as Neo-Confucianism, which was to remain orthodox until the close of the nineteenth century. In the opening decades of the twentieth century it was relegated to limbo by the new currents of thought which were entering from the Occident.

Neo-Confucianism professed to be based on the classics, which Confucian scholars regarded as standard, but it took account of Buddhism and Taoism and was a synthesis which combined Confucianism and the philosophies which underlay these two religions, with Confucianism predominant. The chief formulator was Chu Hsi (A.D. 1130-1200), who, coming late in the Sung, was able to take account of earlier Sung thinkers. Like many of these predecessors, most of his adult years were spent in the service of the state, but in intervals of retirement or of sinecure posts he gave himself to study. His writings, marked by admirable literary style and clarity of thought, did for Confucianism what two centuries later the writings of Thomas Aquinas did for Catholic theology. As Aquinas took account of Greek philosophy, notably Aristotle, who was popular with the intellectuals of the Western Europe of his day, Chu Hsi interpreted Confucianism in the light of Taoism and Buddhism, the other systems with which the Chinese of the Sung were most familiar. Like Aquinas, he dealt with man's understanding of the nature of the universe and of human life. As did many of the Sung thinkers, Chu Hsi gathered about him students in a quiet spot remote from the world and there discussed with them the fundamental problems of philosophy. His views did not win universal acceptance, but for many centuries the majority esteemed them.

A general trend of Neo-Confucianism was toward religious agnosticism. Scholars reared in that philosophy were urbane but religiously skeptical tending to conform to the traditional religious ceremonies with indifferent tolerance. Yet religion did not die. Although Buddhism had passed its peak and was fading in its native India, Buddhist monks still traveled to the historic shrines of their faith and did so until, in the eleventh century, Islam had spread along the caravan routes in Central Asia.

In a variety of other ways the China of the Sung was rich in cultural achievement. Some of the most notable histories of China were written at that time, many studies of individuals, periods, and phases of the past were compiled, and collections of extracts from existing works were made. Publication was facilitated by developments in printing: at their best, the products of the Sung craftsmen in that art equaled any of later centuries. Fiction in the vernacular was composed. Poets were numerous and their creations were voluminous, but their achievements are not generally regarded as equal to the greatest of those of the T'ang. Among the porcelains produced by the Sung potteries are some of the finest ever created. Landscape painting reached heights of supreme excellence. Natural science flourished. Treatises were written on flowers, fruits, astronomy, and medicine which embodied keen observation. In A.D. 1054 astronomers noted the appearance of the supernova from which emerged the Crab Nebula in Taurus. Probably it was under the Sung that gunpowder was first employed in warfare. From the Sung is the first known Chinese reference to the abacus, still a familiar and useful device in reckoning.

The growing commerce was now to quite an extent by way of ports on the coast south of the Yangtze Valley. Improvements in shipbuilding, charts, and the use of the compass facilitated the enterprise of merchants in going overseas for trade, and knowledge of the geography of other lands expanded.

The Mongol Interlude

The conquest of all China by the Mongols which ended the Sung era marked an interlude which was characterized and was followed by striking changes. China was now part of an empire which stretched from the southern tip of Korea into what is now the southern European units of the U.S.S.R., until then the largest empire ever created.

During the relatively few years that it remained intact, the Mongol Empire facilitated travel and commerce in both directions across Central Asia. For example, a Nestorian priest who had been born in North China went to Rome, Bordeaux, and Paris on a diplomatic mission for the Mongols. Many foreigners came to China, among them merchants and missionaries (Franciscans) from Western Europe. Numbers of Italian merchants voyaged to the ports of South China or made their way overland by the caravan routes across the area now known as Sinkiang. Because of the record of his travels written on his return to Europe, the most famous was Marco Polo, who had come as a youth with his father and uncle, Italian merchants, and had entered the employ of Kublai Khan. We hear of a German engineer who aided the Mongols in a successful siege of one of the Sung strongholds. To the Europeans China was very impressive. Cambaluc, the capital which Kublai constructed on approximately the site of the present Peking, must have had a population of at least a million. Marco Polo declared Hangchow, which he saw a few years after it had ceased to be the Sung capital, the greatest city in the world.

The chief permanent contribution of the aliens who came to China at this time was extensive Moslem communities. Christians were few and did not long survive the Mongol rule, but Moslems multiplied and remained, and in the 1960's numbered several millions. In Mongolia the Mongols became Buddhists, but in the present Sinkiang some of the non-Mongol, non-Chinese peoples were converted to Islam. During the Mongol era the present province of Yünnan had a Moslem governor who was followed in that office by a son; other descendants, still Moslem, remained influential after the Mongols were expelled. Under the influence of these officials many of the population of Yünnan accepted Islam and a strong continuing Moslem element came into being. Before, during, and after the Mongol conquest, partly through merchants of that faith, other Moslem communities arose in the ports on the South Coast.

Developments which were presumably of purely native and not of foreign origin were in the drama and the novel. Dramatic performances were not new in China: they had been present from very early times and drama flourished under the T'ang. In Mongol times, however, plays multiplied and from then on were a prominent aspect of the culture. For unexplained reasons the novel also suddenly flowered, though it, too, was not an innovation and had precedents of long standing. It was at this time that some of the most famous of historical romances were written and in a style which approached the vernacular, later to be amplified and put in a more finished form.

The Mongols never fully identified themselves with the Chinese although Kublai attempted to rule as a Chinese Emperor and his dynasty is officially called Yüan. Numbers of Chinese scholars took employment under him and many Mongols conformed to Chinese culture. Kublai honored Confucianism and the descendants of the sage and thereby contributed to the revival of that school in the North. His successors renewed the civil service examinations. Kublai continued policies of the Sung concerning the care of aged scholars, orphans, and the infirm, distribution of food among the poor, and the storing of surplus crops in granaries in times of plenty as a reserve for times of scarcity. He repaired and enlarged the Grand Canal which connected the South with the North, its terminals being the Sung capital, Hangchow, and Cambaluc. It was a means of communication between the South and the North and of conveying the tribute grain from the South to the capital—much as the canal built by the Sui emperors had been a means of supplying their new capital, Ch'ang-an, with food. Yet few Chinese were placed in the high offices, Chinese merchants were restricted to trade with lands to the south and the rest of foreign commerce was turned over to aliens. He forbade the Chinese to carry arms. Many Chinese scholars disdained holding office under the Mongols. They regarded the conquerors as crude barbarians and retired to seclusion. Partly through them the Neo-Confucian tradition was perpetuated and the writings of Chu Hsi were cherished.

Under Kublai the Mongol Empire reached its apex though his attempts to conquer Japan failed, with great loss of life to the Koreans and Chinese who constituted much of the expeditionary forces. Somewhat similarly, attempts to bring Annam, Burma, and Java under Mongol rule did not achieve continuing success.

After Kublai the Mongol Empire drifted apart and its fragments became independent of one another. In China he was followed on the imperial throne by men of inferior ability and most of them with short reigns. The currency was debased, the Mongols issued paper money with insufficient metal reserves and it rapidly depreciated, the realm groaned under heavy taxation, floods of the Huangho added to the distress, revolts broke out and in a prolonged struggle for power a man of humble birth came to the top. He was first prominent in the lower part of the Yangtze Valley and then pressed northward. In 1368 Cambaluc was taken by one of his generals and in that year he was proclaimed Emperor of a new dynasty.

The Ming Dynasty

The new dynasty inaugurated in A.D. 1368 had the designation of Ming, meaning "brilliant" or "glorious" and in part it deserved the title. In contrast with the Yüan and the dynasty which followed, it was a purely Chinese regime—the last until the Republic of China and the People's Republic of China. It established its rule over more of China proper than had any dynasty since the T'ang, making its weight felt in Mongolia, parts of the later Sinkiang and Manchuria, and overseas in the South as far as Ceylon. Under its earlier reigns the Empire was prosperous, wealth increased and much building was undertaken, both by the state and on private initiative. Never before, and, indeed, never again until the twentieth century, did Chinese ocean-borne commerce range as far as in the initial decades of the fifteenth century. Art and literature flourished, some philosophical and scholarly activity was seen and the forms of government developed by the Ming persisted, with some changes, into the opening years of the twentieth century.

Yet under the Ming China did not register as important achievements as under the Han and the T'ang. Culturally in the Ming period the Chinese genius was far less creative than in the Chou period, during the Han and the T'ang, and even the Sung. In that important respect the Chinese were beginning to mark time. Whether from a reaction against the alien intrusions under the Mongols or for other reasons, institutionally and culturally under the Ming, China was conservative. Elaborating what had been inherited from pre-Mongol days, but doing far less that was new than in earlier eras. Nor territorially did the Ming attain the territorial control of the Han and the T'ang.

The first Ming Emperor was thirty years on the throne. He re-established order after the near anarchy of the last years of Mongol rule, renewed the civil service examinations, constructed an imposing capital at Nanking, on a site in the lower part of the Yangtze Valley which had been used for that purpose by some earlier states, and ordered the creation of an Empire-wide system of schools in which the curriculum would be based on the Confucian classics.

The death of the first Ming Emperor was followed by four years of civil strife over the succession to the throne but out of it emerged, as the third Emperor of the Ming, one of his sons, a monarch under whom the dynasty reached its apex. That monarch established his capital at Peking and there, overlapping in its northern section the ground covered by Cambaluc, he constructed the imposing city which, unaltered in its main outlines, is the capital of the People's Republic of China. Although the Communists have erected new buildings, have constructed great factories and apartment houses outside the walls, and have refurbished the imperial palaces and maintained the tradition established by the Republic of China of opening them to the public, architecturally Peking remains what it was under the Ming, one of the most impressive capitals—in the judgment of many the most impressive capital—in the world. The third Ming Emperor pursued an aggressive foreign policy. He dispatched military expeditions into Mongolia, occupied much of Annam, and some of the tribal chiefs in Burma accepted his authority. The Shogun who was the dominant official in Japan acknowledged him as suzerain. He sent several naval expeditions to the south and southeast—to Cochin-China, Java, Sumatra, Cambodia, Siam, India, and Ceylon—and several of the princes in these lands recognized his overlordship. A ruler in Ceylon who behaved rudely was captured and brought to Peking, and it is said that for a half century part of that island paid tribute to the Ming.

After the third Ming emperor had been gathered to his fathers the vigor of the ruling house declined. No monarch occupied the throne whose achievements equaled those of the founder of the dynasty and his son. Outside China proper the influence of the Empire declined. Annam resumed its independence and tribute from dependent states lapsed. Wars with the Mongols recurred and during one of them the attackers carried off the Emperor and the Chinese were constrained to renounce all intervention in Mongolian affairs. Japanese pirates raided the coasts and looted important cities. The Japanese attempted the conquest of China by way of Korea, and although they did not succeed in marching beyond the Yalu, in the peninsula itself they defeated a Chinese army. From time to time famine took its toll.

On the whole, however, under even the later Ming, China was prosperous and important cultural developments occurred. In the earlier decades of the Ming, population mounted. Structures in honor of Confucius were a familiar feature of the cities. They were now called halls rather than temples, thus reducing their religious significance. The change was at least partly due to the prominence of the Neo-Confucianism of Chu Hsi, the philosopher who was now esteemed to be the orthodox interpreter of Confucianism. Confucianism was emphasized in the civil service examinations, and the format of these examinations continued into the first years of the twentieth century, and through them the bureaucracy was recruited. The scholar class from which officialdom came was committed to Confucianism and through the prestige which accrued to it Confucianism was increasingly standard in the mores of the population as a whole and was dominant in Chinese culture. Some scholarly dissenters from Neo-Confucianism emerged, an indication that originality was not entirely stifled. Others endeavored to curb the corruption which was sapping the administration of the Empire. Printing continued to facilitate the production and the wide circulation of literature. Encyclopedias—chiefly excerpts from existing books—were compiled, the largest of them by imperial direction and so huge that its publication daunted the exchequer and it existed only in a few manuscript copies. However, most of the voluminous writing was pedestrian, showing more diligence than creative originality—local geographies and histories, works of reference, commentaries on existing works, and treatises on law and medicine. Painting and ceramics were produced in great quantity and with elaborate technique, but little with the genius which had characterized the Sung. Examples of Chinese ceramics were widely distributed through overseas commerce and were carried as far away as the Near East and Europe. Much construction was seen of bridges, city walls, and temples. Some was of high quality—as in the palaces and temples in Peking—but earlier examples largely provided the models: little departure was seen from traditional forms.

Of major importance were renewed contacts with Western Europeans, on the initiative of Europeans. The Ming dynasty was a contemporary of that expansion of Western European peoples that had its first foreshadowings in the Crusades and the medieval commerce of the Italian cities. In the nineteenth and twentieth centuries that expansion was to work the basic revolution in Chinese culture which was the outstanding feature of the history of the Middle Kingdom (as China has been known) in the twentieth century. The Ming dynasty was only a little over a century old when the voyages of

Columbus brought the Spaniards to the Americas. Coincidentally the explorations along the coast of Africa directed by Prince Henry the Navigator culminated in the rounding of the Cape of Good Hope by the Portuguese and the establishment of Portuguese trading stations in India, the East Indies, and Malacca. After several preliminary expeditions, in 1564 the Spaniards began the occupation of the Philippines which was to add those islands to their empire. A half century earlier, probably in 1514, Portuguese traders reached the China coast. In the latter half of the sixteenth century they acquired the foothold at Macao which they retain to the present day.

Through these contacts came contributions which were eventually to have profound effects on China. The silver which entered from Mexico probably augmented the trend to a money economy which was one of the features of the Ming years. From the Americas tobacco was introduced and new foodstuffs—chiefly maize, peanuts, and sweet potatoes—which under the next dynasty contributed to a prodigious growth of population. The propagation of Christianity was renewed, initially and chiefly by Jesuits through Macao, but eventually by Roman Catholic missionaries of other orders, mainly Spaniards by way of Manila.

The Manchu Invasion

In the first half of the seventeenth century the decadent Ming were swept over by a fresh invasion of aliens, Manchus, from the North. They conquered the entire Middle Kingdom and extended the borders of the Empire over the outlying regions. In so doing they expanded their realm over more territory than had been occupied by any preceding dynasty and gave a precedent for the imperialistic ambitions of the Republic of China and the People's Republic of China. Under them, too, China's population multiplied far beyond any previous totals. In the eighteenth century China was the most populous realm on the face of the globe. In this respect it surpassed all the other contemporary empires—Spanish, French, Russian, Ottoman, British, and Mogul. Its system of law and order was fully the equal of any and surpassed most and perhaps all of them, for that was before the humanitarian movements of the nineteenth century had improved conditions among Western European peoples. It probably had a greater volume of printed books than had all the rest of the world.

The Manchus were related racially to the creators of the Chin dynasty. Early in the sixteenth century an able leader welded them into a strong political unit and many Mongols were incorporated into their ranks. Their head assumed the imperial title and called his dynasty Ch'ing, the name by which it was to be known throughout its history. The Manchus had often attempted the invasion of China proper, but not until internal revolts had weakened the Ming did they succeed in establishing themselves in Peking. In 1644 a rebel captured that city and the Ming Emperor hanged himself. Aided by Chinese generals, the Manchus defeated the rebel, took possession of the capital, and slowly pushed south the stubbornly resisting supporters of the Ming aspirants to the throne. Not until 1662 did the last die—in mountain fastnesses in the Southwest.

Even before they had eliminated the Ming, the Manchus were adopting Chinese culture. Although to the very end of the dynasty they kept somewhat aloof from the Chinese and retained several of their old customs, they maintained the Ming laws and institutions and associated the Han Chinese with themselves in the administration of the Empire. They required the male Chinese to shave the fore part of their heads and grow queues—the Manchu tonsure—as a sign of allegiance to the Ch'ing. When, in 1911-1912, the Manchus were ousted, queue-cutting was a symbol of liberation.

Not until 1681 was the Manchu rule firmly established. The first Manchu to reign in Peking came to the throne as a minor and died in 1661, in his twenties, the year before the death of the last Ming to claim the throne. His successor, usually known by the designation of his reign period as K'ang Hsi, also was put on the throne as a minor, at the age of seven. Although he theoretically reached his majority in 1667 at the age of thirteen, not until 1669 was he able to break the power of the regents.

The K'ang Hsi Emperor proved to be one of the strongest monarchs in China's long history. He reigned until 1723. A contemporary of such outstanding Western rulers as Louis XIV and Peter the Great, he was fully as able as either of them. He was devoted to hunting, traveled extensively in his domains, was diligent in his duties, and professed to have at heart the welfare of his subjects. Like the greatest of the Emperors of preceding dynasties, he was not content to defend China proper against the incursions of the border peoples who were chronically seeking to invade the fertile valleys and plains to their south, but brought them into subjection. He enforced his claim to be suzerain of the entire confederation of Mongol tribes; he conquered much of the present Sinkiang; his troops installed a protégé in Lhasa and he stationed garrisons at strategic points in Tibet and on the roads between that country and China. Thus for the first time he brought that highland under Chinese rule, a step which was to serve as a precedent for the measures taken by the People's Republic of China in the 1950's and 1960's.

In the days of the K'ang Hsi Emperor the contacts which Europeans initiated with China in Ming times increased. With his characteristic vigor, the K'ang Hsi Emperor checked a Russian attempted penetration of his borders. The Tsar's subjects were then making the advance across the northern reaches of Asia which brought that vast area under the sway of Moscow and establishing outposts in territory on the northern borders of Manchuria which the K'ang Hsi Emperor regarded as his domain. In 1685 his troops took Albazin, a Russian foothold, and carried its garrison to Peking. After desultory fighting a treaty of peace was negotiated (1689), the first between China and a European power. Here was a foreshadowing of the recurring tensions between Russia and China which were to punctuate much of Sino-Russian relations in the nineteenth and twentieth centuries, and, unlike these latter, with the advantage resting with Peking. Catholic missionaries continued to come to China and from time to time were met with persecution. For some years the K'ang Hsi Emperor was disposed to favor them, especially the Jesuits who were in Peking, for he was interested in features of European art and learning which the Jesuits were introducing as a means of commending their religion to the Chinese intelligentsia. He used the Jesuits as interpreters in his negotiations with the Russians. However, when a dispute arose—the "rites controversy"—over the attitude of the missionaries toward some Chinese customs, he acted in a fashion that foreshadowed the policies of the Communists in the 1950's and 1960's. At the instance of Jesuits who sought his opinion on the points at issue he differed sharply from the decisions of the Papal see, and irritated by the obedience given to Rome by the missionaries, he gave the latter the hard choice of conforming to his judgment or leaving his domain: he would brook no compromising of his authority by a foreign ecclesiastic. Some Jesuits who found a way of salving their consciences in sidestepping the Pope's decree and obeying the Emperor's command remained in Peking, but the imperial policy reinforced by later emperors slowed the growth of Christian communities and by the opening decades of the nineteenth century seemed about to work their extinction.

In his domestic policies the K'ang Hsi Emperor was equally vigorous. He sought, unsuccessfully, to abolish the Chinese custom of binding women's feet, strove to improve the currency, to lighten taxes, and to promote honesty and efficiency in the bureaucracy, and subsidized scholarship. For example, under his auspices a dictionary was produced which remained standard into the twentieth century. He maintained the civil service examinations. He studied the Confucian classics, and by his famous "Sacred Edict" attempted to encourage Confucian morality and to discourage his subjects from conforming to Buddhism, Taoism, or Christianity.

The Manchus who followed the K'ang Hsi Emperor on the throne were not the equal of that monarch. The one who most nearly approached him was his grandson, best known as the Ch'ien Lung Emperor, who reigned from A.D. 1736 to his abdication in 1796. He, too, was able, intelligent, hard-working, fond of the chase and outdoor life, and a patron of the arts and literature. He prided himself on his skill as a poet, calligrapher, and painter. In ability to rule effectively he seems to have compared favorably with Catherine the Great of Russia and Frederick the Great of Prussia, the outstanding European monarchs of his day. Under him the Ch'ing Empire reached its apex. He rounded out the Ch'ing domains in the West and gave to them the designation of Sinkiang ("the New Dominion"), and, setting a precedent for Communist practice, moved into it Chinese colonists from the neighboring provinces of China proper. He quelled an uprising in Tibet and strengthened his control in that region, thus setting another precedent for subsequent Communist actions. His armies compelled Nepal to accept his suzerainty, laying the basis for the claims of the Republic of China and the People's Republic of China. In the Southwest and the western borders of Szechuan he reduced the non-Chinese tribes to subjection, compelled Burma to recognize him as suzerain, and constrained the rulers of Annam to receive investiture from Peking and to pay "tribute" to the Ch'ing. Treaties with Russia in 1768 and 1792 further regulated the still exiguous relations with that country. British and Dutch embassies seeking commercial concessions were treated as coming from "tributary" states and failed in their objective. In the Ch'ien Lung period the population of the Empire mounted to about 300,000,000 by the end of that era. Partly to take advantage of the new food plants from the Americas more uplands were brought under cultivation. As a result, because of improper methods of tillage, much of the newly cleared land was badly eroded and left unfit for crops, and the danger of floods mounted. But this unhappy aftermath was not immediate.

Largely through the writings of missionaries, Europeans acquired a great admiration for China. In Western Europe Chinese porcelains and sedan chairs became popular, wall paper was introduced, Chinese silk and fine cottons were the vogue, and tea was extensively imported.

Toward the end of the reign of the Ch'ien Lung Emperor the condition of the realm began to deteriorate. In the later years an unscrupulous favorite became the chief minister, amassed vast wealth, and corruption in the bureaucracy was rampant. The Emperor who succeeded to the throne confiscated the possessions of the favorite, suppressed the revolts which had broken out, and attempted to reduce extravagant expenditures in the court and the peculations of officialdom. He slowed but could not prevent the progressive decay, which was soon aggravated by the impact of Western peoples in the nineteenth and twentieth centuries. It was in the second reign after that of the Ch'ien Lung Emperor that the impact began to be acute.

Culturally the great years of the Ch'ing dynasty were marked by the volume of art and literature that was produced but little of it was creative or new. The civil service examinations were maintained and with them the education that was preparation for them. In philosophy, on the other hand, significant new currents were seen. A few thinkers, dismayed by the conquest of the Empire by a people whom they regarded as "barbarians," sought the cause for what to them was disaster. They ascribed it to the dominance of the Neo-Confucianism of Chu Hsi, and some creators of what was called the Han Learning endeavored to bypass the commentaries on the classics written by the Sung thinkers and return to the original texts.

Chinese Culture Prior to Occidental Impact

At the outset, it should be noted that from the beginning of the Ming dynasty very little basically new had been achieved in Chinese culture. Innovations had occurred in several aspects of the Empire's life and institutions, but fundamentally the China of the mid-nineteenth century was the same as that of the China of the end of the fourteenth century. Had a Rip van Winkle begun his sleep during the reign of the third Ming Emperor and awakened under the second successor of the Ch'ien Lung Emperor, in some respects he would have felt very much at home. True, he would have noted that population had more than doubled, that many new temples, palaces, bridges, and city walls had been erected, and that the volume of printed books had mounted. Had he been peculiarly observant, he might have been aware of some importations from abroad, chiefly new food plants, tobacco and pipes, a few buildings in European style in the imperial summer palace in the western suburbs of Peking, astronomical instruments of European design on the Peking wall, and large cannon cast under European direction. However, in most literary circles he would have heard the same subjects discussed and found the same standards of excellence as when he had fallen asleep. The new paintings and ceramics would have conformed to familiar standards, and except for the quaint structures which gave variety to the summer palace, architecture would not have perceptibly changed. He would have found Manchu garrisons in the chief cities, the queue worn by boys and men would have startled him, and so would have changes in the style of clothing. But these, while significant, would not have been basic.

The reasons for the static condition of Chinese culture at the mid-nineteenth century must be in part conjectural. As we have repeatedly remarked, again and again in the pre-Ming centuries striking changes had been seen. Many were evidence of marked creativity: some were due to importations from other cultures. But the last brilliant era had been that of the Sung which had been terminated by the Mongol conquest late in the fourteenth century. One possible explanation of the conservatism was the reaction against foreign rule expressed in a marked ethnocentrism. More plausible was the effect of the civil service examinations. These examinations were revived by the Ming and continued by the Ch'ing. They were stereotyped, were based upon the Confucian classics as interpreted by Neo-Confucianism, and prized literary style rather than creative thought. Success in them brought prestige to the individual, his family, and his village or city, and they led the road to office under the government, power, and wealth. Education was directed toward preparation for them and thus shaped the Chinese mind, perpetuated a rigid conservatism, and nourished a pride which viewed all other cultures as uncivilized and their peoples as barbarians who at their best might have developed amusing mechanical devices.

Since the revolution stimulated by the impact of the Occident was marked by an emphatic rejection of much of the inherited culture, if we are to understand that revolution we must be aware of what was repudiated. As we have suggested, the repudiation was not complete. Many features of the older culture, including administrative divisions, the characters used in writing, art forms and even more basic attitudes survived and governed the new China which emerged.

Government under the Ch'ing

Government, a major achievement of the Chinese, was an important aspect of the culture of the old China which was in part swept aside by the revolution. The governmental structure was not the creation of the Ming or the Ch'ing, but was the product of a long evolution. To it many emperors and statesmen had contributed. With occasional interruptions, it had held together as large an area and as numerous a people over as long a stretch of centuries as any ever developed.

At the apex of the government was the Emperor whose authority, in theory, was absolute and given by the mandate of heaven. He was expected to set a worthy example to his people, and if he or his successors failed to set that example, heaven would withdraw its mandate and confer it on some other man and his house. A sign of heaven's displeasure might be floods, droughts, or some other natural disaster, for to the Chinese mind, earth, heaven, and man constituted a whole and the welfare of man depended upon the harmonious cooperation of the three. By his "virtue" the Emperor could obtain the cooperation of heaven and earth and so ensure the well-being of his subjects. The Chinese were practical-minded. As they saw it, a successful rebellion—for each dynasty had been founded by one— was evidence that Heaven had transferred its mandate. The Emperor was the religious head of mankind, and either in person or by proxy officiated at such ceremonies as those at the altar of heaven in the imposing structures immediately south of Peking and at the altar of earth to the north of the capital. He also appointed or confirmed the heads of the various cults and promoted or demoted gods. In principle he appointed all members of the official bureaucracy in the capital and the provinces.

In practice the Emperor's power was limited. A few men of abounding energy, such as the K'ang Hsi Emperor, could carry the heavy administrative burdens, but men of mediocre ability or of lesser physical strength had to delegate their duties or let them go by default. Custom, precedent, and the inertia of officialdom limited even the strongest monarchs, officials could petition the Emperor expressing criticism or suggesting positive actions, and a board in the capital had as its responsibility keeping watch over the Emperor and his officials and reporting delinquencies and even taking exception to the deeds or lack of action of the monarch himself.

In Peking were various other boards, each with specific functions, some executive, some judicial, and some legislative. In contrast with Western governments, no ministry of foreign affairs existed: the Chinese could not conceive of the possibility of a family of reciprocally independent nations of equal legal rank. To their mind civilized mankind could have of right only one government, that with the Emperor as its head.

Below the central government in descending order were provinces (eighteen during much of Ch'ing times), prefectures (called *fu*), districts (*hsien*), and some other subdivisions. The heads of all these administrative units were recruited through the civil service examinations, were appointed from Peking, and were responsible to Peking. To reduce the danger of rebellion, with rare exception no official was assigned to his native province, appointments were usually for three years and were seldom renewed for more than an additional three years before transfer to another post, and by various checks and balances officials were set to watch one another.

The civil service examinations were held at stated intervals and led to "degrees." There were three major degrees; only the successful candidates in the lowest of the three could sit for the second, and only those who had passed the second could enroll for the third. For each degree many more were examined than could be passed. When the government was short of funds, some degrees could be purchased, but no such prestige attached to degrees acquired in this fashion as to those awarded through the competitive channels.

Local government had in it much of group responsibility. All the members of a village, family, or even a city could be held accountable for the deeds of any of its members. Village government was by a council of elders, in theory nominated by their fellow villagers and confirmed by the magistrate, but who might come to the position in other ways—among them tacit recognition by public opinion. Leading the council was a headman.

The system of law differed from that in Western countries and was frequently a source of friction with foreigners. For instance, men were often held responsible for accidental deaths and as a penalty were required to compensate relatives or submit to fines or corporal punishment.

Government revenues were chiefly from cash taxes on land, tribute collected on produce, imposts on foreign trade and domestic commerce, profits on the state monopoly of the manufacture and sale of salt, levies on various commodities, and, at times, the sale of offices.

Under the Ch'ing the military organization was far from efficient. It was made up in part of the descendants of the Manchus, Mongols, and Chinese who had assisted in the conquest of the country. In addition was a force of Chinese troops, larger than the other, but, to prevent revolt, so divided into diverse units that they could with difficulty be combined to face foreign invasion. For the most part they were poorly paid and still more poorly disciplined. Officers were recruited through examinations but not nearly as gruelling or with the same subject matter as those for civil officialdom.

Under an able monarch of unusual physical vitality—notably the K'ang Hsi Emperor—the complicated wheels of the state were kept running with a degree of efficiency. But as men of lesser stature came to the throne the machinery creaked or broke down, corruption became rife—both in the central administration and on the local level —and inefficiency and unwillingness to assume responsibility permitted laws to go unenforced and needed repairs in canals and dikes to be neglected, with the crippling of transport and disastrous floods as an aftermath. Moreover, under the best of monarchs tenure of office was uncertain. Because of cabals at court even the ablest official might be demoted or allowed to commute by suicide the disgrace of a death sentence.

Life and Manners

Basic in the old China was the family which constituted a mutual aid and protective association, especially in villages and rural districts. The family was expected to care for its aged and its ill, to provide schools for its children, and to settle disputes among its members. In some sections the many ramifications of the family constituted a kind of clan. Many families lived together in large compounds in which several smaller units of husband, wife, and children were members and were presided over by a patriarch or, on occasion, a matriarch. Yet most households consisted of the husband, wife, and children. Many clans had ancestral "temples" in which the tablets of deceased members were kept, graded according to generations and in honor of whom ceremonies were periodically conducted. Family lineage was important, and many could trace their descent through several centuries. Frequently an individual would claim to belong to the province of his ancestors even though he and his immediate forefathers had not lived there for a number of generations. The importance of the family was symbolized by the fact that in writing the name of an individual his patronymic came first and was followed by his given names.

Marriage was chiefly for the purpose of continuing the family line and thus ensuring the perpetuation of the honors paid to the ancestors. This meant that marriages were arranged by the elders and not by the couple immediately concerned. Betrothal might be in the childhood of the pair and be almost as binding as marriage—the marriage to be consummated as the couple reached adolescence. The couple might not see each other until the wedding, for social intercourse between the sexes was discouraged after childhood.

Since the family name was carried on through the male line, boys were more highly prized than girls; thus formal education in literature was usually only for them. Some girls were literate, but education of women was mostly in the duties of homemaker and was imparted by the mothers. The lot of women was at times very unhappy. The practice of binding the feet of girls was almost universal, and for the most part only the Manchus, the very poor, and the Hakkas, a distinct group in the South, did not conform to it. It was a social convention of long standing and a girl was disgraced if she came to maturity with unbound or large feet. The process of binding was very painful, and although the suffering became less acute when the foot had been reduced to the desired dimensions, walking remained difficult.

By the Confucian tradition ethics were largely centered on the family. Of the five basic social relations inculcated by that system, three had to do with the family—father and son, elder brother and younger brother, and husband and wife. Duty to one's parents included both father and mother, and children were urged by their conduct to honor their parents and do nothing to bring them sorrow. Elder brothers had duties to their younger brothers, while the latter were supposed to defer to the former. Ideally a husband treated his wife as thoughtfully as he would an honored guest. Human nature being what it is, strains frequently developed within families. A husband might take a concubine, perhaps to satisfy his physical cravings, perhaps to obtain the son which his wife had failed to bear, or, having been born, had died. Mothers-in-law could make miserable the lives of daughters-in-law. Yet Chinese society owed much of its continuing cohesion to the family.

Related to the emphasis on the family was the traditional Chinese respect for age. Whether man or woman, the septuagenarian and the octogenarian were paid especial honor, and this was particularly true if there were children, grandchildren, and great grandchildren. Birthdays were occasions for congratulations and presents. Many widows who had not remarried and were noted for their virtue were publicly commemorated by ornamental archways appropriately inscribed.

In addition to the family, the Chinese had many other forms of organization. Secret societies flourished. Several continued for centuries and from time to time one or more of them fomented insurrections. Under the Republic of China membership in such societies was important in national politics. Some secret societies were not only mutual protective associations but as well levied blackmail on outsiders to attain their ends.

Guilds played a large part in Chinese life. Some were composed of merchants, others of employers and employees organized by particular crafts. Still others were of beggars, of the blind, and of thieves. They could bring collective action to protect the interests of their constituents or to enforce their will. In large cities merchants from a province or another city constituted themselves into guilds. Still other associations were formed for particular purposes—among them ones by farmers for the protection of crops or for cooperation in irrigation, and others to pool resources for such expenses as burials. Benevolent societies, largely of Buddhist origin, were maintained for such objectives as providing soup kitchens and lodging houses for the needy, supplying coffins for the poor, and conducting hospitals and schools.

Chinese society under the Ch'ing did not know such hard and fast class lines as did some other societies. The Indian caste had no parallels. Earlier dynasties had been marked by hereditary aristocracies, but by the Ming and Ch'ing these had largely disappeared among the Han Chinese. The Ch'ing had a few noble families, mostly Manchus, and some Chinese as well. Although notable public achievement might be rewarded by honorific titles which passed from father to son and the ancestors of the possessor might be posthumously decorated, usually the title died with the recipient or if passed to the descendants was in a progressively lower rank with each succeeding generation. Some families had a tradition of culture and education and because of the advantages which these gave, the sons were better prepared for the civil service examinations and so for official posts. But on the whole much mobility was seen. By ability and character men of lowly birth could win recognition and rise to the highest positions in the state.

Gradation in social status was in part by occupation. In theory scholars came first and teachers were considered objects of reverence —along with heaven, earth, the Emperor, and parents. Next came farmers, for they produced the food on which the nation subsisted. Artisans were third, for they also were producers. Merchants were low in the social scale, for they subsisted on other men's toil. Officials were ranked with scholars, for they were recruited from the educated through civil service examinations. But intermarriage between families of officials and wealthy merchants was not unknown, for each profited by the alliance—the officials in wealth and the merchants in social standing.

Some occupations and groups were held in disdain—among them were soldiers, beggars, actors, prostitutes, eunuchs, underlings to officials, and slaves who were a minority and were chiefly servants in well-to-do households.

Social Customs

As in every society, conventions were developed for social intercourse which eased tensions and facilitated amenities. Some were based upon the ancient classics of the Confucian school and others on age-long practice. The disregard of these conventions by Westerners was regarded by the Chinese as a mark of a barbarian and as evidence that the Westerner was outside the pale of civilization. "Face" was important. To cause another to "lose face" was the height of discourtesy. The equivalent of "face" is an almost universal human trait, but the Chinese seem to have been more sensitive to it than some other peoples. It was associated with their intense pride as a people. Connected with "face" was the large part played by middlemen. In occasions involving possible dispute and loss of "face" a go-between could be employed to effect a settlement entailing compromise of conflicting interests. Possibly related to "face" was the dislike for physical violence. The Chinese looked upon it as a lack of good breeding. But, to cause an antagonist to lose "face," an aggrieved party in a dispute might commit suicide. Public opinion would hold the other responsible and might compel him to make reparation to the victim's relatives and to pacify the officials. Also related to "face" was a dislike for bluntness and abruptness in social intercourse. Requests were often made indirectly or subjects of possible embarrassment were merely hinted at—trusting the other party to understand without a direct statement.

Etiquette was elaborate, requiring deprecating reference to anything connected with the speaker and praise of everything associated with the person addressed. The guest was seated at the left of the host and good form required the guest to protest his unworthiness, especially if others were present, and to accept only with great show of reluctance. Affability in social intercourse was required and any departure from it was considered boorish. A host might detest his caller, but custom decreed that any indication of his inner feelings was a sign of bad breeding. Spoons and chopsticks were used in eating. Custom governed the giving and receiving of gifts and indicated which proportion of what was offered should be accepted and what should be offered in return. The drinking of tea was a part of every social call or business conversation. Garb was carefully prescribed for every occasion.

Under the Ch'ing the Han Chinese did not engage in games requiring physical exertion. Athletics of the Western kind were considered beneath the dignity of the scholar. That had not always been true: for example, in T'ang times polo had been played.

For diversion the Han Chinese had many games of skill. Gambling was common. The tea shop was a favorite center for fellowship and gossip. There the professional storyteller regaled the patrons with his narratives. The theater was a universal form of diversion, with the larger towns and cities having buildings devoted to it. Temples were frequently used for dramatic performances, even of a purely secular nature. Peripatetic theatrical troupes visited the periodical markets. The Chinese theater had its distinct conventions which were understood and, if well carried out, appreciated by the audience. The themes of the plays were often historical, the Confucian virtues were extolled, and vice was condemned. Through the theater accordingly, the masses acquired much of their knowledge of history—even though fictionalized—and of the orthodox virtues. Jugglers, acrobats, and sleight-of-hand experts, many of them very skillful, also provided entertainment.

Festivals and special days helped to break the monotony of life. The most important was that of the New Year. In theory all debts were supposed to be paid before that day. The season was marked by cessation of all but the most necessary work, by feasting, by family gatherings, and by social calls. Children made their obeisance to their parents, and pupils paid their respects to their teachers. Although birthdays were observed, at the New Year a year was added to the reckoning of the age of each member of the family. Since a child was regarded as a year old at its birth, after its first New Year its age was reckoned as two years.

In the spring the chief festival was Ch'ing Ming, especially devoted to commemorating the dead by cleaning and repairing the graves and by offerings before the ancestral tablets and the graves. The Dragon Boat Festival came on the fifth day of the fifth moon and may originally have been associated with the summer solstice. It marked the apex of the good influences of the *yang*, or male element, associated with the sun, and the beginning of the decline toward the *yin*, or female element, identified with darkness and evil. Precautions were therefore taken against the evil spirits which were believed to bring disease. In some places the day was marked by "dragon boat" races, theoretically in search of the dead body of a statesman of the later years of the Chou who was said to have committed suicide by drowning. The seventh day of the seventh month was the festival of the herdsman and the weaver maid and was especially devoted to women. Also in the seventh month was the festival for the departed spirits, when the latter, who were supposed to have returned for a time, were formally escorted back to their customary abodes. The harvest festival came in the eighth month and was very much for the children. The ninth day of the ninth month was an occasion for picnics. The last festival of the year was at the winter solstice, and on it the Emperor sacrificed at the altar of heaven and honors were paid to ancestors.

Religion

The family and religion were intimately connected, for many religious ceremonies were observed in the home.

Under the Ming and the Ch'ing religion had a long history and contained elements from many stages of its development. The Chinese were usually said to have three religions—Confucianism, Taoism, and Buddhism. But not all religious beliefs and observances were embraced by them. The Chinese were very eclectic in their religious beliefs. Only relatively few were exclusively devoted to any one faith: most of them were Buddhist or Taoist monks. Even the Confucian scholar did not confine himself to the observances in honor of that sage. To some degree the Chinese were also tolerant. From time to time religious persecutions had broken out: some of the most

severe had been instituted by Emperors, usually more for political
or economic reasons than from strictly religious motives. Probably
back of the toleration was a basic uncertainty—doubt as to which if
any of the religions were true and the desire to profit by whatever
advantages came with any or all of them. In general, too, the Chinese
believed that by a moral life and the faithful observance of ritual
evil could be warded off and rewards of varying kinds obtained. The
universe was assumed to be trustworthy and to be on the side of
virtue; therefore the moral life and the faithful observance of prescribed ceremonies were believed to further the well-being of those
who conformed to them, both in this life and in whatever life lay
beyond the grave. The observance of religious and moral duties was
held to promote the prosperity of the individual, of the family, of
the community, and of the Empire.

Under the Ch'ing and to a degree under the Ming, what we call
Confucianism had the support of the state. The K'ang Hsi Emperor
had formulated sixteen sententious moral maxims which were later
elaborated in a vernacular version and were ordered to be publicly and
regularly read and taught. They extolled the Confucian virtues and
warned against Buddhism, Taoism, and Christianity. Although some
religious rites were encouraged in Confucianism, opinions have differed as to whether Confucianism was a religion. The Chinese name
for it is *K'ung Chiao* (Confucian Teaching) or *Ju Chiao* (the Teaching of the Learned). Confucianism taught that the Emperor was
the religious as well as the political head of the state since upon him
depended in large part the beneficent cooperation of the universe
with man and he was held to be the Son of Heaven and the asso-
ciate of Heaven and Earth. He could admit, promote, and demote
divine beings in the official pantheon and upon him devolved the
duty of performing the religious ceremonies which furthered the
smooth coordination of the universe with man. The chief of these
ceremonies was at the altar of heaven where at the longest night in
the year he sacrificed to heaven, in the presence of representations
of the imperial ancestors and various divinities and forces. Many spirits and divinities were honored by the Emperor and by officials within
their jurisdictions. Each territorial division had a building or group
of buildings devoted to Confucius and the leading exponents of
Confucianism in various ages. In them were tablets to these worthies,
and in some a statue of Confucius. In each of these structures ceremonies were celebrated officially twice a year and by rites and cos-

tumes believed to be those used in the Chou era. At the home of Confucius were the grave and a temple of Confucius of which a descendant of the sage was the custodian.

Among other deities honored by the state were the god of the walls and moats, for which each city had a temple, as for a tutelary divinity; gods of the soil and grain; the god of literature; and the god of war. There were also temples to the Emperor. The state also honored the spirits supposed to be associated with sacred mountains, and of these, T'ai Shan, in Shantung, was the most revered.

Associated with Confucianism were the honors paid to ancestors, for the weal or woe of the dead was supposed to be dependent on the living. The home of the eldest son and, usually, of the other sons had tablets to a deceased father and mother before which incense was burned daily, on stated occasions offerings of food were made, and important family events were announced. The ancestral temples of the clans in which were tablets to the ancestors were maintained by endowments.

Under the Ming and the Ch'ing, Buddhism, although in a slow decline since the T'ang, continued to be prominent still with hundreds of temples, monasteries, and shrines and many thousands of monks. Support came from endowments in land, from offerings of the faithful, and from fees for the performance of ceremonies. Many of the monasteries and temples were in picturesque sites on mountains and were embowered in groves of stately trees. They had statues to various Buddhas, bodhisattvas, and gods, and some had representations of the heavens in which the faithful were rewarded and of the hells in which the wicked were punished. Buddhism encouraged pilgrimages to its sacred mountains. It had an enormous literature, some in the form of popular tracts for the laity.

Taoism had temples and shrines which showed the influence of Buddhism, but it was not as prosperous as that faith and was also in a slow decline.

Whether the ceremonies connected with the ancestors should be classified with religion may be and has been debated. Certainly for many, perhaps for the majority, they were in that category. The observances associated with the ancestors were universal since widespread conviction was held that the welfare of the living depended in large part on the faithfulness of each generation in maintaining the ritual ordained by custom. The sceptical could argue that since from time immemorial the ceremonies had been part of the Chinese way of life, to continue them was essential if civilization as the Chinese conceived it was to be preserved.

The vast majority of the Chinese, even among the educated, held to beliefs which, although in practice all four incorporated them, were not an integral part of Confucianism, Buddhism, Taoism, or the cult of the ancestors. They included a popular polytheism, animism, and a conception of the way in which the universe is organized and could be made to serve the welfare of men. The polytheism contained the many gods recognized by the state. It also embraced deities which entered from a variety of channels and which might ultimately be accorded endorsement by the state. For the overwhelming majority of the Chinese the existence of evil spirits or demons—*kuei* as they were called—was axiomatic. The kuei had many forms and many sources. They might be in such objects as trees, clothes, mountains, stones, and leaves. The dead might become kuei—including suicides, the victims of accidental deaths, and mothers who had perished in childbirth. If so, they could not be released from their suffering until they had lured one of the living to a similar demise. Kuei could take the form of animals, or, as an animal, assume the shape of a beautiful woman and, having won the embrace of some man or youth, turn and kill him. Responsibility for misfortunes to individuals or groups—such as sickness, insanity, bad crops, or insect pests—was attributed to kuei. Many ways were devised for guarding against kuei or expelling them if once they were in possession.

Many of the methods of assuring protection against the kuei or of defeating them were associated with a dualism which was believed to be integral in all nature. As we have suggested, that dualism was identified with the *yang*, the male principle—and the *yin*, the female principle. The yang prevailed in the gods, in fire, the sun, light, good deeds, males among men and animals, and certain plants, trees, and fruits. The yin was present in darkness, the earth, the moon, evil, and the female sex. Numbers of means were employed to enlist the yang against the kuei—among them charms, Buddhist monks, and Taoist experts.

Closely related to the yang and yin was what was known as *fêng-shui*—literally "wind" and "water." Fêng-shui had back of it the conviction that every locality has acting upon it forces which are advantageous or disadvantageous to human welfare. Among them are yang and yin. They govern structures which men erect—whether graves, houses, temples, palaces, or cities and the fêng-shui of every site must be determined, for the welfare of a family, a group, or a city depends upon the choice of a site with features which conform to the demands of that pseudo-science. Experts were called in to select such sites and treatises were written to guide them. An unpropitious site might be improved by adding features that are lacking or by removing those which are adverse. Thus the misfortune or success of a family might depend upon the fêng-shui of ancestral graves, and the success in the civil service examinations of the sons of a city was sought by erecting pagodas which improved the fêng-shui.

Economic Life

By the time of the Ming and the Ch'ing the economic life of China was already varied and the result of long evolution. Cities and villages abounded, with the specialized trade and industry which had brought them into existence and which continued to keep them alive.

In general, the attitude of the state toward economic life combined freedom for individual initiative with regulation by the state and with government monopolies. Thus the government exercised a monopoly of the production, distribution, and sale of salt, undertook public works, such as dikes to control streams and prevent floods, and canals to further the transportation of grain to the imperial capital and for other purposes. It accumulated cereals in times of plenty to equalize supplies in periods of scarcity. It undertook relief of the poor during famines. It regulated some businesses. Yet for the most part individuals and groups were given freedom in their economic undertakings.

Agriculture absorbed the energies of the majority of the population. That was necessary if food, tea, and raw materials—silk and cotton fiber—were to be produced in sufficient supply for China's millions. Agriculture was by the intense application of human labor. Some mechanical devices existed which facilitated that labor—such as plows, sickles, flails, hoes, and simple means of bringing water to the growing crops. But the operation of all of them entailed the use of men's muscles. The units of cultivation were generally small. Surveys early in the twentieth century disclosed that farmers were seeking to make a living on tracts which varied from an acre to twelve acres. The larger averages were in the North, where the rainfall was less than in the Yangtze Valley and the South. Difficulties due to small acreage were heightened by the fact that the holdings of an individual were often made up of smaller tracts separated from one another, sometimes, at distances. Landed estates existed, some as endowments for temples and others as possessions of landlords, resident or absentee. The proportion of the cultivated soil embraced by them differed from province to province. In some places it was small, in others fairly large; the "land reform" carried through by the People's Republic of China confiscated and redistributed considerably less than half of the arable land.

The rural problems which confronted the China of the Ch'ing period were many and staggering. In addition to landlordism were extreme crowding and soil erosion due to inefficient methods of cultivation. The most densely peopled rural sections had more inhabitants to the square mile than rural Japan or Bengal, the most thickly settled area of India. In clearing uplands to take advantage of the new food crops introduced from the Americas in Ming and early Ch'ing times, forests were cleared from thousands of square miles and eventually the humus was washed away. It was to the solution of these problems that the Communists addressed themselves.

However, the Chinese farmers had displayed great skill in utilizing the soil and conserving and improving fertility. They cultivated a wide variety of crops. They raised many legumes and thus enhanced the nitrogen content of the soil. Several grains supplied much of their food—wheat and millet in the North and rice of many varieties in the Yangtze Valley and the South. Vegetables were a large part of the normal diet. Traditionally dairy products, such as butter and cheese, were not consumed, and less meat per capita was consumed even than in Japan, with its similar rural economy. But protein was obtained from bean curd, fish, pigs, and chickens. Fish were to be had from the sea, streams, and irrigation ponds, and therefore from sources which did not encroach on the cultivation of the soil. Indeed, the thrifty farmer fish stocked the artificial pools from which he obtained water for his crops during the growing season, drained them after the harvest, and reaped his harvest of fish. Pigs and chickens were in part scavengers which fed on what human beings did not use. Fats were obtained from vegetable oils. Thus the needed proteins and fats were from sources which did not necessitate the maintenance of such animals as cows which fed on what can otherwise be human food. In several ways the farmer obtained fertilizers. He made extensive use of "night soil," of the droppings of animals, of green manure, of ashes rich in potassium and phosphorus, of rotation of crops, of earth from canals, presumably rich in needed minerals, and of sun-dried bricks which had outlived their usefulness in buildings and, pulverized, were spread on the fields. Often crops of differing maturing times were sowed in alternating rows on the same plot. Ingenious mechanical devices were developed. The bamboo, available for food, tools, and buildings, was extensively grown. These many methods did not necessarily presuppose deliberate and scientific study, but were obtained through experience over many centuries and were handed down from generation to generation.

As in the rest of the world before the Industrial Revolution, industry was in the handicraft stage. Flourishing in towns and cities and tending to be grouped by localities and streets which specialized in one or another product, it was organized by guilds which made possible cooperation and curbed wasteful competition.

Domestic and foreign trade and commerce were through small units, and here also guilds were a prevailing form of cooperation which fixed prices and maintained standards of quality. In thousands of villages, too small for guilds, markets were held periodically and even daily to which came buyers, sellers, and numerous peddlers. As in medieval Europe, weights and measures varied from place to place and from commodity to commodity. Honesty was insured by the custom of having guarantors for an individual who could be held accountable if the latter defaulted or cheated.

Across the centuries the Chinese had had many currencies—from cowries in Shang times to paper money under more than one dynasty. Under the Ch'ing the only indigenous coin was the copper cash, which in various forms had been employed for many centuries. For larger units of value the Chinese employed small ingots of silver which the banker or merchant tested for fineness and which might be cut into smaller sections. Under the Ch'ing, and especially in its later years, many kinds of silver dollars were imported, most of them from Mexico, but some of other origins. As with weights and measures, much variety and confusion existed, with differing exchange rates from one form of currency to another and in foreign transactions.

Extensive use was made of banks, which were all private. In the nineteenth century the most extensively represented were the Shansi bankers who took their name from Shansi and had their headquarters there. Family banks, their owners and employees were mainly from that province and they worked in close cooperation with one another.

Many other kinds of banking enterprises existed: pawnshops; "cash shops" whose primary function was changing money from one kind to another; others which more nearly corresponded to Western banks in that they received deposits, made loans, bought and sold drafts, and issued bills which served locally as money.

Transportation was by various methods, much on rivers and canals by boats of many kinds moved by sails, oars, the current, and by men who pulled them from the bank. Much was by road: in the North, four-wheel vehicles were common; in the Yangtze Valley and the South more was by wheelbarrows and, for passengers, by sedan chairs. Inns were numerous. Postal service for official business was through government channels. For non-governmental purposes it was through private agencies: most of them covered one, two or three provinces. Yet in its efficiency, or lack of it, the transportation of China in the Ch'ing dynasty compared favorably with the rest of the world before the nineteenth century.

Chinese language must be considered as having two distinct aspects: the spoken and the written. The spoken language has many dialects. The most widely spread has been what foreigners call Mandarin. Its standard has been that of the capital, Peking. In various forms, all of them mutually intelligible, except in some rural districts, it has prevailed over most of the North and West and in some areas south of the Yangtze River. In the coastal provinces from the mouth of the Yangtze southward, several dialects have existed which are reciprocally unintelligible. As we have seen, both the Republic of China and the People's Republic of China have sought to overcome that obstacle to national unity by teaching in the schools the kuo-yü, or national speech, a standard form with Mandarin as its basis.

The written language has had two forms. One is the classical or literary style, which foreigners called *wên li*. It experienced many developments and was a living language. It was that employed by scholars in the Chou period and possibly took form first in Shang times. As compared with the other form, the vernacular, it is highly condensed and with its own syntax and grammar. It appeals to the eye rather than the ear, and when read orally apart from visual contact, unless it is a familiar passage, even the scholar might not be able to understand it. All respectable scholarship used it, and both prose and poetry were composed in it. The vernacular utilizes the same characters as the classical or literary style, but though much of the older literature employed it, especially under the Ming and the Ch'ing, scholars viewed it disdainfully. It remained for the New Tide or Renaissance of the 1920's to give the vernacular literary stature.

In the older China literature and learning were highly esteemed. In such respect were they held that paper with characters written or printed on it was kept from dishonorable uses, and incinerators were placed on streets for the reception and burning of discarded fragments.

As we have indicated, traditional China was extraordinarily rich in literature. From the Sung dynasty onwards that literature had been reproduced by printing and at the dawn of the nineteenth century, as we have said, in sheer volume China had more books than all the rest of the world. That literature had many forms—among them histories, local and Empire-wide, on special aspects and periods and covering all the course of the Empire, essays, philosophy, religion, poetry, geography, descriptions of travels, science, and fiction.

Education was centered on preparation for the civil service examinations. Families who could afford them employed tutors to instruct their sons or several families might join in hiring a teacher. In theory teachers were highly respected, but in practice they suffered from inadequate pay and uncertain tenure. None were specially trained in pedagogy. In elementary schools the curriculum consisted in memorizing texts, many of them from the classical books and quite beyond the comprehension of the child. As a result Chinese scholars had phenomenal memories and could quote at length entire books. Later in the course commentaries were studied and memorized. More advanced schools trained in composition and provided models for essays. The emphasis on memory gave the educated a command of standard literature and, since the books employed were those esteemed by the Confucian school as canonical, an intimate knowledge of Confucian philosophy and ideals. However, an unhappy result was a narrow outlook, an intellectual pride, and a bigotry, which dismissed as uncultured learning not of the Confucian tradition. Here was a poor preparation for the reception of the new knowledge which came with the irruption of the West in the nineteenth and twentieth centuries.

Art and Architecture

A major feature of the civilization of China before the revolution wrought by the incursion of the West was the art and architecture that had been created. Here, as in several other aspects of the culture of the country, the achievement was unique.

An important contribution to the world as a whole was in ceramics. China, the name by which porcelain was popularly known in the Occident, is continuing evidence of that aspect of Chinese cultural achievement. As we have seen, true porcelain ware appeared at least in the T'ang period and a proto-porcelain much earlier. As in much else in the art of the country, quantities of the best porcelain were produced in the Sung era. The Ming and the Ch'ing dynasties saw mounting quantities, increased perfection in technique, and an elaboration of designs and of the use of many colors. Whether they equaled the Sung in artistic quality is debatable.

A continuing contribution to mankind was silk and silk fabrics. At least as far back as the Han, silk, both in its raw form as thread and in textiles, was a major export. Even after the rearing of silkworms and the manufacture of silk were introduced to other countries, silk long remained prominent in the commodities sold to the West.

In the eighteenth century Chinese gardens were the inspiration of some forms of landscaping in the West. In a different category was the debt of the West to China in wallpapers.

Major unique accomplishments of the Chinese genius were in painting. The Chinese artist did not equal the Western artist in the delineation of character in portraits, but much earlier than in the Occident high levels were reached in landscapes. Painting was by the brush pen which was used in writing, and line was valued. Calligraphy, through the use of the brush, was esteemed a fine art. In painting the Ming and the Ch'ing artists largely followed the precedents set in the T'ang and the Sung, and their achievements did not equal those of the earlier periods.

Chinese architecture was also distinctive. In its temples, its palaces, and its city walls it displayed a sense of proportion with its courtyards, its quiet dignity, its balancing of roofs and walls, and its use of color which were congenial to the Confucian tradition. Bridges were utilitarian, had unobtrusive solidity, and, in arched examples to permit the passage of boats, displayed a poised grace that was typical of other major structures. Pagodas, of Buddhist provenance, were developed into one of the impressive features of urban architecture and in many instances crowned hills in a fashions which punctuated the landscape and accentuated the sense of proportion without violating it.

In other aspects of the aesthetic—as in bronze objects, in sculpture, and in the use of jade—the Chinese genius found expression in distinctive ways.

In painting, ceramics, and architecture China's immediate neighbors paid that Empire the compliment of imitation. This was especially evident in Japan and Korea. The Japanese and Koreans were not content with uncreative reproduction and placed the stamp of originality on what came to them from China.

In the broad categories of science and mechanics, the achievements of the Chinese are well known—papermaking and the spread to the West of that aid to the dissemination of ideas; the invention of printing approximately six hundred years before Gutenberg; the use of the mariner's compass centuries earlier than in Europe; and gunpowder. Not so widely appreciated are Chinese discoveries in mathematics and astronomy, the early awareness of sunspots, novae, super-novae, and variable stars; the catalogues and maps of the stars; the records of earthquakes; and the use of mirrors and lenses.

Abrupt Transition

At mid-nineteenth century Chinese culture appeared to be intact as a product of a continuous development extending over more than three thousand years, destined to go on a course which had long been pursued. Changes had been seen, at times rapid. Outside influences had entered and had given rise to alterations, some of them striking. Yet patterns established before the Christian era persisted. For about four centuries the rate of change had been slowing, but new movements had appeared, evidence that creativity had not been completely stifled. However, the major contributions from other cultures, notably Buddhism and the art forms and philosophies which accompanied it, had been assimilated, and their influence, while still present, was waning. Confucianism, dating from at least the sixth century B.C., was more potent than at any previous time and dominated Chinese thought and institutions. Although it had been repeatedly modified and dissent was not unknown, in the form it had had in the Sung period Confucianism governed the ideals and set the standards for the scholar class through which the Empire was ruled. Because of the prestige and the power of that class it permeated the millions of Han Chinese who constituted the vast majority of the population.

Now, in the mid-nineteenth century, came a series of events un-

precedented in the varied history of China. A quite different civilization, the West, encroached upon the Empire, and the result was
abrupt transition and a revolution which swept aside much of the
traditional culture. Observers who watched the change were fasci-
nated and at times bewildered, for the spectacle was what might have
been expected had denizens of another planet invaded the earth,
bringing with them an utterly alien way of life, dynamic and overwhelming.

The change was rendered the more traumatic by the fact that
Western civilization was itself undergoing a profound revolution, a
revolution which in part was produced by the very forces that later
shaped the new China of the mid-twentieth century.

All peoples of the world were affected by the impact of the West;
however, in no other highly developed civilization were the changes
as much felt as in China. Not even in India, with a civilization as
old as China's and a population almost as large, was the impact as
sweeping. Nevertheless, it should be emphasized again that though
the impact of the West was traumatic and brought many changes,
many basic atittudes and cultural achievements persisted from China's
great past and helped to determine the pattern of the emerging
revolution.

THREE

THE TRAUMATIC IMPACT OF THE WEST

The civilization responsible for the traumatic changes in China's culture was that of the Occident or the West—Europe and its extension in the Americas, notably in the United States and to a lesser extent in Canada. Western civilization was even older than that of China, for it had its roots in the Tigris-Euphrates Valley, Egypt, and that "Fertile Crescent" which constituted a bridge between Mesopotamia and the Nile. To it had come striking contributions from the Jews, the Greeks, and the Romans.

Not until late in the fifteenth century did European peoples play a major part in the non-European scene. To be sure, under Alexander the Great the Greeks had penetrated to Central Asia and Northwest India, but their contributions to India and China had been slight. The Roman Empire had dominated the Mediterranean and lands which fringed that body of water, but except for some commercial contacts, relatively insignificant, the peoples of that realm had had little effect upon the great cultures in India and China—lands that in wealth, population, and civilization could be compared with the Roman world. In the days of Mongol rule a few Europeans made their way to China, but their effect was slight.

In the fifteenth century European peoples began that expansion which culminated in political domination of the world and cultural effect on all mankind in the nineteenth and twentieth centuries. Spaniards and Portuguese were pioneers by way of the seas. In the seventeenth century they were followed by the English, the Dutch, and, to a less extent, the French. Contemporaneously the Russians were moving across the vast reaches of northern Asia.

As we have seen, in the Ming and the early Ch'ing periods Europeans were continuously visiting China. However, except in the introduction of tobacco and new food plants from the Americas, the cultural effects were slight. Roman Catholic missionaries arrived, but attracted only a few thousand converts. Culturally they made some contributions, chiefly in astronomy and mathematics, but the inherited culture of China remained undisturbed.

Shortly before the middle of the nineteenth century the impact of Europeans began to assume dimensions which were to have revolutionary effects. That impact arose from developments among European peoples which were in themselves revolutionary, such as the Industrial Revolution with growth in manufacturing and the search for markets and raw materials. Another development, closely related to the first, was growing wealth. Still another was the century of peace which followed the termination of the Napoleonic Wars, a century broken only by such relatively brief conflicts as the Crimean War, the battles connected with the unification of Italy, the Seven Weeks War, and the Franco-Prussian War. The Civil War in the United States was more destructive but lasted only four years. Democracy, in its Anglo-Saxon form, was growing. Amazing advances in science were being achieved, with an enlarged understanding of the physical universe and the constant improvement in transportation and communications through the steamship, the railroad, the telegraph, and, later, the telephone, the automobile, the radio, the airplane, and television. Medicine and surgery were revolutionized. Striking contrasts were seen in religious thought: on the one hand Marx and Engels were writing *Das Kapital* with its anti-Christian note, religious skepticism was rife, and anticlericalism was vocal; on the other hand a marked revival of Christianity occurred in both the Roman Catholic Church and in Protestantism.

The nineteenth century was marked as well by a renewal and rapid growth of empire-building by Western powers. In the mid-nineteenth century the British conquest of India was completed, while earlier the British emigration to Australia and New Zealand had begun and British settlement was being pushed westward in Canada. The French were building an empire in North Africa and Indo-China. The United States was extending its territory to the Pacific and its citizens were settling California, Oregon, and Washington and were filling the gaps between those frontiers and the Mississippi. Russia was strengthening its outposts in Siberia, had occupied Alaska, was moving into the trans-Caspian region in Central Asia, and was threatening British power in India. Europeans explored Africa south of the Sahara and in the last quarter of the century divided it among themselves. Similarly the British, French, Germans, and, latterly, the Americans were parceling out the islands of the Pacific.

Paralleling the empire-building and the colonial expansion of European peoples was the rapid increase of Christian missions among non-European peoples arising from the quickened life in the Roman Catholic and Protestant churches, and, although to a much lesser extent, in the Russian Orthodox Church.

Mounting Pressure on China

China could not hope to escape the impact of this expanding Occident and its revolutionary movements, though for years the Chinese authorities failed to appreciate its significance and attempted to keep their doors tightly closed against it. Foreign merchants were confined to a narrow strip of land on the waterfront in Canton where they lived in what were called their "factories." Their commerce was through a group of merchants, the Co-hong, who enjoyed a government-authorized monopoly and through whom Westerners were required to have all their dealings with the officials. Regular diplomatic relations were nonexistent, for Peking regarded the Europeans as barbarians and could not conceive of the possibility of treating their governments on the basis of equality. They were, so Peking held, outside the pale of civilization. The Chinese and Manchus assumed as axiomatic that no other state could dispute the pre-eminence of the Middle Kingdom, insisting that foreign merchants and foreign sailors must be subject to Chinese law and Chinese courts. The Chinese government fixed the tariffs and port duties to be levied on foreign goods. The monsoonal character of the winds and the fact that the foreigners still had only sailing ships meant that slack seasons existed in foreign trade; at such times Europeans usually took refuge in Macao, which, with its few square miles and tolerant Portuguese administration, provided a welcome haven.

The English had the largest share in the foreign trade with China. After the defeat of Napoleon they ruled the seas, the Industrial Revolution had begun in Great Britain, wealth there was mounting, and markets were sought for the products of the power-driven machines, especially cotton. The English were not long content with the Chinese restrictions on their commerce.

The revival of the Christian missionary movement was beginning to make itself felt. Roman Catholics were reinforcing their missionary staffs, depleted by prolonged persecution, the French Revolution, and the Napoleonic Wars. Although forbidden by law, small Christian communities existed in several parts of the Empire, and missionaries, coming by way of Macao, surreptitiously made their way to them. Protestants had no such footholds, though a few of their missionaries found residence in the Canton factories, there studied the language, and prepared literature in it while others sought access to the overseas Chinese in Siam, the East Indies, and Malacca.

Unfortunately for China, mounting pressure from the West came at a time when the Ch'ing was repeating the experience of other dynasties and was crippled by declining vigor at the top. The Empire was ill-prepared to meet the challenge. A well-meaning incompetent, vacillating and irresolute, was on the throne. Heading a structure in which everything ultimately depended on the monarch, he had neither the native ability nor the experience to deal vigorously and intelligently with as great a test as had ever confronted the Empire. Officialdom, ignorant of the trends in the world at large, including the Occident, and serenely confident in the superiority of Chinese civilization, could not be expected to deal intelligently with the new conditions.

The First Anglo-Chinese War

The initial breach in China's self-imposed isolation was precipitated not by the basic issue of foreign trade and international relations in general, but by the effort of the imperial government to prevent the importation of opium. The smoking of opium was a relatively recent development in China. Not until the early eighteenth century had it become serious enough to attract official attention. Then attempts were made to prohibit it, but by the 1830's opium constituted the bulk of the foreign imports. Western merchants had been seeking commodities which would be in demand in China and which they could exchange for the tea and silk that constituted the main exports. China was so self-sufficient economically that Europeans and Americans could hitherto cover the margin between exports and imports only by extensive shipments of silver, which was often difficult to obtain. To them opium, produced chiefly in India and Turkey, constituted the answer. Until 1834 the English East India Company had a monopoly of British trade with China, but in that year the monopoly ceased and many independent British firms and enterprising business men entered what had the promise of large profit. When the East India Company sought to restrict the production of opium in the territories under its control, supplies of the drug came from sections of India not yet ruled by the English. Much was imported through Canton, much also was smuggled through other ports with the connivance of venial officials. Peking was not only distressed by the deleterious effects on the morals and health of the addicts, but was alarmed as well that the reversal in the balance of trade and the outflow of silver were responsible for a change in the price level and consequent suffering among the masses. Late in 1938 the Emperor appointed a special commissioner to end the traffic once and for all, a Chinese of marked ability who by sheer merit had risen from the ranks. As governor-general over two provinces he had shown energy in fighting opium-smoking and curing addicts in his jurisdiction. In 1839 he arrived in Canton and set about his task with his accustomed vigor, ordering all the opium in foreign hands to be surrendered and commanding the foreigners to give their bond to refrain from engaging in the traffic. To enforce his demands, he stopped foreign trade and had the foreigners confined to the factories until they obeyed. The foreigners surrendered their supplies of the drug and a few signed the required bond. The opium thus confiscated was destroyed.

The issue was complicated by a clash between British and Chinese conceptions of law. In a fray between British sailors and Chinese, one of the latter was killed. The British superintendent of trade declared the death accidental but compensated the relatives of the deceased, and a British court meted out punishments to some of the sailors involved. The Chinese insisted that the men be turned over to them for trial. The English refused, the Chinese cut off their trade, the English merchants took refuge in Macao, and, when the Portuguese authorities declined to protect them, withdrew to the then barren and sparsely populated island of Hong Kong.

Hostilities broke out in November, 1839. They were suspended from time to time by negotiations and were almost entirely naval attacks by British ships on Chinese ports along the coast and the lower Yangtze. They were brought to a climax in July, 1842, by the British capture of Chinkiang, the city on the south bank of the Yangtze where the Grand Canal reached that river, and by the slaughter of the Manchu defenders. Thus communications between the North and the South were threatened and traffic on the Yangtze was stopped. The British forces moved on to Nanking and presumably would have taken that city but for the timely surrender of the

Chinese. The Ch'ing military and naval organization had proved inadequate to meet this new kind of attack from the sea.

From the British standpoint the real issue was not opium but Chinese unwillingness to deal with Europeans on the basis of the international law which the latter had developed. The Chinese believed the crucial controversy to be over the right of their government to prohibit the importation of the drug. To them, and to the world at large, the hostilities have been known as the "Opium War." However, the basic question was the right of the Empire to set the terms on which intercourse with other governments would be conducted and this issue remains a bone of contention. Down to World War I foreign powers dictated terms; thereafter Chinese resistance mounted, and under the People's Republic of China Peking succeeded in resuming and maintaining the pre-treaty policy.

The war of 1839-1842 had a significance which the Chinese of that day did not recognize and which the English saw but dimly, if at all. Until that time, as we have seen, the chief threat of invasion had come from the land frontiers—on the northeast, north, and northwest. Against it successive dynasties had set their defenses, partly by constructing and maintaining the Great Wall and, under more vigorous rulers, by mastering the peoples in these areas. The menace from these directions continued—in the nineteenth and twentieth centuries chiefly from the Russians. Now, however, the major challenges were from the southern and eastern seas—first from Western Europeans and then from the Japanese—against whom the Chinese were slow to set up effective opposition. In the mid-nineteenth century they viewed them much as they had the Japanese pirates who from time to time had troubled the coasts, as "barbarians" who could be dealt with as such. The Ch'ing, the Republic of China, and the People's Republic of China all failed to develop fleets to meet the sea-borne threat. Nor did the latter two, in the era of aviation, construct adequate air forces. As a result, in the 1930's and 1940's Japan almost overwhelmed the country and but for the United States might have succeeded in fully doing so. In the 1950's and to the time that these lines were written, the People's Republic of China resumed against the marine menace much of the policy of isolation which characterized most of the Ming and Ch'ing eras.

The treaties which followed the first Anglo-Chinese war set the precedent for later ones exacted by the Western powers from the reluctant but impotent Ch'ing. The document known by the name of Nanking, which was dated August, 1842, and signed, symbolic of China's defeat, on board a British ship of war, had as its chief provisions: (1) the opening of five ports—Canton, Amoy, Foochow, Ningpo, and Shanghai—for the residence of British merchants and their families, with a consular agent in each to be a medium of communications between the Chinese officials and the merchants; (2) the cession to Great Britain of the island of Hong Kong; (3) compensation by China for the opium confiscated and the imprisonment and threatened death of the British subjects and superintendent of trade and for the expenses incurred by the British armed forces; (4) the release of all British subjects imprisoned at the time in China, and, similarly, the release by the British of any prisoners held by them; (5) the publication by the Chinese of a schedule of fair and fixed import and export duties and the promise that transit dues to the interior of China would not exceed a certain percentage of the value of those goods; and (6) the promise that correspondence between British and Chinese officials was to be on the basis of equality and without the assumption by the Chinese that the former were interior to the latter. In 1843 a further Anglo-Chinese treaty was signed which fixed the customs dues and thus established the precedent that China could not alter them without British consent. It also guaranteed that British subjects should enjoy the privileges of the most favored nation.

Several other Western powers having commerce with China quickly took advantage of the British victory and entered into treaties with China. The treaty with the United States, signed in 1844, opened the same five ports to the residence and commerce of American citizens, specified regulations for trade, and elaborated the provisions for the extraterritoriality which had been hinted in the British treaties but not defined. In the American document extraterritoriality was made to entail the punishment by Chinese officials of Chinese subjects guilty of criminal acts against American citizens and the trial and punishment by American authorities of Americans guilty of crime against Chinese. Extraterritoriality was also extended in part to civil cases. By the most favored nation clause, extraterritoriality as defined in the treaty with the United States applied also to British subjects. In 1844 the French obtained a somewhat similar treaty, and late that year the French were responsible for an imperial edict which permitted the erection of Roman Catholic churches in the open ports and the acceptance of that faith by Chinese. In 1845 a decree extended the same privileges to Protestants, and a year

later, another edict confirmed the toleration of Roman Catholicism
and promised the return of some of the churches erected during the
reign of the K'ang Hsi Emperor which had since been confiscated.
In 1845 Belgium obtained a treaty and that was followed in 1847
by one with Sweden and Norway. In 1851 a treaty with Russia
further regulated the trade which had been authorized and regulated
in the seventeenth and eighteenth centuries.

The War with England and France

In the years which immediately followed the first group of treaties
the pressures of the expanding West on China mounted. Steam
navigation was facilitating trade. The United States acquired California (1848), and in 1849 the discovery of gold attracted miners and
merchants by the thousands. Settlers were pouring into the Oregon
country. Commerce across the Pacific rapidly increased. Chinese
laborers were attracted to the California mines and also were being
recruited for British Guiana, Peru, and Cuba. The importation of
opium continued. On Hong Kong a thriving commercial community
was developing, and Westerners were moving into the five ports
opened by the treaties. In Canton they met determined resistance
and their residence was still confined to the factory district on the
river front. Shanghai, earlier a sleepy little city, was rapidly out-
stripping Canton as the main center of foreign residence and commerce. Situated as it was on a small stream near the mouth of the
mighty Yangtze, it was the natural approach of Westerners to the
commerce of that vast valley. Outside the narrow area enclosed by
the city walls, the British, Americans, and French established communities. A few years later (1863) the first two were combined for
administrative purposes into what was known as the International
Settlement. Missionaries, both Roman Catholic and Protestant,
increased in numbers. Around the same time (1853-1854) Commo-
dore Perry constained the Japanese to sign their first treaty with a
Western power and so opened that country to the West.

With the pressures, friction inevitably arose. In the eyes of the
Chinese the treaties of the 1840's, exacted at the mouth of the
cannon, had granted too much, but the foreigners regarded them as
merely preliminary to what was needed if their relations were to be
placed on the footing which they expected with other countries. The
American and French treaties provided for revision at the end of
twelve years and in 1856 the American representative attempted to
gain a revision. The British, under the most favored nation clause,

made a similar demand. But to both requests the Chinese would not accede. Anti-foreign riots broke out in some of the ports, especially in Canton, and the Chinese authorities found them difficult to prevent or suppress. Piracy, rampant along the coast, troubled Chinese as well as foreigners. Chinese officials were reluctant to treat their foreign opposites on the basis of the equality specified in the treaties and on occasion were rude and arrogant.

In 1856 the English and the Chinese drifted into war. The initial incident that provoked hostilities was what the English interpreted as an insult—the hauling down of the British flag on a ship under Hong Kong registry and the arrest of the crew. At first, fighting was confined to Canton where the Chinese destroyed the foreign factories and carried out further actions against the aliens, while the English retaliated and took and dismantled some of the forts. The murder of a French Roman Catholic missionary early in 1856 provided the French with an occasion for joining the English. Because of the Sepoy Mutiny in India (1857) the English delayed in pressing their demands. Moreover, the French and the English had not yet recovered from their exertions and sufferings in the Crimean War (1854-1856). The Russians, still licking the wounds inflicted on them in that struggle, did not collaborate with their recent enemies but were quite willing to take advantage of any opportunity to press their interests in China. The United States did not wish to join in the war, but late in 1856 the Americans sought redress for an insult to their flag by dismantling the offending forts near Canton. Late in 1857 British and French forces took Canton.

In 1858 the English, French, Americans, and Russians sent notes to Peking asking that foreign envoys be received in Peking and permitted to reside there, that more ports be opened to trade, that foreigners be allowed to travel in the interior, that the customs tariff be periodically revised, that inland transit dues of foreign merchandise be regulated, that piracy be suppressed, and that the persecution of Christians cease. The replies proved unsatisfactory. The British and French fleets went north to enforce their demands and took the forts which commanded the approach to Tientsin, the main seaport of Peking. With his capital threatened, the Emperor yielded, and the same year treaties were negotiated and signed at Tientsin with Great Britain, France, Russia, and the United States. The treaties with the first three powers provided for the exchange of ratifications at Peking. When, in 1859, the Russian and American representatives arrived on the coast for that purpose, they achieved it, although the American was subjected to some humiliation. The British and the French ministers insisted on proceeding by way of Tientsin instead of the route prescribed by the Chinese. That route was one assigned to envoys of tributary states and to accede would be tantamount to accepting a subordinate position and thus negating one of their principal demands—that of full equality with the Chinese. In their effort to go by Tientsin in 1859 they were repulsed; thereupon they renewed the war. The following year they returned with strong re-enforcements. With these they seized Tientsin and pressed on to Peking. In taking Peking they destroyed the summer palace west of that city in retaliation for the disregard of a flag of truce and the death of several of the force which bore it. The exchange of the ratifications of the treaties of Tientsin was then accomplished and additional conventions were forced from the Chinese. The ruins of the summer palace continued to remind the Chinese of the loss of face in the British and French capture of Peking, and into the twentieth century they were a source of irritation which intensified the Communists' denunciation of Western imperialism. The British commander had hoped that the action would teach the Chinese a lesson in international law as the West understood it. It had the opposite effect: the Chinese assumption that they were dealing with "barbarians" was heightened. For the time being they might have to temporize, as they had again and again in earlier centuries when faced with invasions of non-Chinese. But their conviction of cultural superiority was heightened rather than weakened. The leaders of the People's Republic of China continued to cherish it, although the ideology which they espoused was not that of the traditional China.

The Treaties of 1858-1860

The treaties which China was constrained to accept as a result of the foreign aggression of 1856-1860 went far beyond those of the 1840's in compromising the independence of the Empire and in undermining its inherited culture. The features of the treaties which contributed substantially to the revolution produced by the impact of the West were: (1) New ports were opened to foreign residence and commerce, some on the Yangtze River as far inland as Hankow, and three on the coast in the North—one in Manchuria, one in Shantung, and Tientsin. They made possible the permeation of regions not opened by earlier treaties, for the five specified in these documents and the cession of Hong Kong to Great Britain were on the coast south of the Yangtze and not in the North or the interior. (2) Foreign merchant craft were given permission to use the Yangtze, thus furthering the penetration of the interior. (3) Ministers and ambassadors of the treaty powers and their entourages were to reside in Peking and be received as representatives of independent states, not tributary to China but legally fully equal with that Empire. (4) Foreigners were free to travel anywhere in the interior. (5) Kowloon, a bit of the mainland opposite Hong Kong, was ceded to Great Britain. (6) The regulations for extraterritoriality were elaborated. (7) In a new schedule of tariffs a duty was placed on opium; thus the importation of that drug was legalized. (8) Freedom for the propagation of the Christian religion, previously subject solely to Chinese permission, was written into the treaties. Christians, both foreigners and Chinese, were guaranteed freedom to practice their faith and liberty to proselytize among the Chinese. So far as their religion was concerned, Chinese Christians were thereby removed from the jurisdiction of their government and were placed under the protection of foreign powers.

The Chinese text of the French treaty—which the Chinese said was not official but upon which the French insisted—gave Roman Catholic missionaries the right to rent and own land outside the treaty ports, and in practice this privilege was extended to Protestant missionaries. The non-Chinese character of Christianity and the association with foreign imperialism were thus emphasized—a circumstance which was to be a chronic source of hostility and on which the extreme nationalists were to capitalize under the Ch'ing, the Republic of China, and the People's Republic of China. The treaty structure capped by the documents of 1858-1860 remained substantially unaltered for nearly sixty years and formed the legal basis for China's foreign relations until it was challenged by events connected with World War I. It was not completely negated until World War II.

Foreign powers, notably Russia, took the opportunity afforded by China's weakness to encroach on the Empire's territory. The British annexation of Kowloon embraced only a few square miles and was a logical corollary of their possession of Hong Kong. In 1858 China ceded to Russia all its territory north of the Amur and agreed to the joint occupancy of the land east of the Ussuri. In 1860 joint occupancy was terminated and the region east of the Ussuri was given to Russia. At the time, this concession did not seem seriously to compromise China, for few if any Manchu or Han Chinese were in the area; however, it was a retreat from the position of the K'ang Hsi

Emperor, and late in the nineteenth and in the twentieth century was followed by the attempt of the Russians, both under the Tsars and the U.S.S.R., to control all Manchuria. In the southeast, France was pursuing the advance begun in the eighteenth century which was soon to remove Tongking from its intermittent but traditional incorporation in the Chinese Empire.

Threatened Political and Economic Chaos

When they obtained their treaties from the imperial authorities, the Western powers had no intention of weakening the Chinese government but simply wished to obtain access to the markets of the country and civilized treatment of their representatives and nationals. To their mind, by their blindness the Chinese were refusing to join the family of nations and had to be taught to observe normal regulations and courtesies. Nineteenth-century Westerners knew little of the Empire, and the admiration which Europeans of the Enlightenment had conceived for China and its civilization had largely been eclipsed by what merchants and diplomats were now reporting. Yet, when the realm seemed to be about to disintegrate, their self-interest in conserving and developing a market for their commerce led some of their diplomats to seek to shore up the regime in its struggles to avoid collapse.

At the outset of the 1860's that collapse seemed imminent. With the triumphant approach of the British and French forces on Peking, the Hsien Fêng Emperor, who had come to the throne in 1851, fled and took refuge in the Ch'ing country resort in Jehol about a hundred miles north of Peking. There, despairing and humiliated, he gave himself up to dissipation and died in 1861 at the early age of thirty, without naming his successor. Some of his ministers placed his five-year-old son on the throne, and a distracting struggle for the regency ensued.

Internal economic conditions were deteriorating. A few years earlier the population was reported to have been 400,000,000, the highest in the history of the Empire. The pressure on subsistence mounted, and unrest was rife. In 1853, in a disastrous flood, the Huangho changed its course from an outlet south of the Shantung Peninsula to which it had been held for about six centuries to an earlier channel north of that mountainous province. As we have seen, by its heavy sedimentation it chronically built up its bed above the surrounding plain, and by extensive public works the state had sought to confine it to its course by reinforcing its natural dikes. But in the declining efficiency of the imperial regime the dikes had not been sufficiently maintained and much of the money appropriated for them had gone to line the pockets of corrupt officials. The change of the course of the Huangho and the accompanying floods brought death to thousands.

Even more serious were rebellions. The one which most threatened the Ch'ing dynasty was the T'ai P'ing Rebellion, led by a Chinese who had come in touch with Protestant missionaries and had adopted a garbled form of their faith. Its leaders held to a compound of Christian teachings and indigenous beliefs and practices. The T'ai P'ing movement attracted many who were discontented with existing economic conditions, others who craved adventure, and still others who hoped to profit by it as an opportunity for plunder. Largely an uprising against landlords, rich peasants, and merchants, in the twentieth century many Communists looked upon it as the beginning of the revolution of which their part was the climax. Initial hostilities appeared in the South, in Kwangsi Province, in 1848, and fighting became serious in 1851 and 1852. In 1853 the T'ai P'ing forces moved northward and then down the Yangtze to Nanking, capturing that city and making it their capital. Had their leader been competent, they might have overthrown the Manchus and established a new dynasty with him as the first Emperor, for that was their professed purpose, but the leader was a visionary, a religious fanatic, and more and more a victim of megalomania. The rebels introduced some reforms which might have proved salutary, but their record was mostly one of destruction and the net result was the devastation of some of the fairest sections of the Yangtze Valley.

Other rebellions included the Nienfei, in the north, a Moslem uprising in Yünnan, in the southwest, and one in the northwest that for a time threatened to wrest Sinkiang from the Ch'ing.

The Ch'ing Wins a Reprieve

For a few years in the 1850's and 1860's the demise of Ch'ing seemed imminent. The combination of incompetence at the top, widespread corruption, natural disasters, mounting population, helplessness before European aggression, and internal revolt appeared to presage both the end of the dynasty and chaos. The experience was not new; several earlier dynasties, among them the Han and the T'ang, had been in similar peril and had been given an extension. But never before had China been called upon to face the irruption of as potent a culture as that of the Occident. Her most perspicacious statesmen were not even dimly aware that the Empire was being engulfed in a revolutionary world. Sweeping change might be postponed but was inevitable. Attempts to prevent it could result only in more drastic collapse.

Late in the 1860's and in the 1870's and 1880's able Manchus and Chinese won a seeming reprieve. The heir to the Hsien Fêng Emperor, known as the T'ung Chih Emperor, was an infant. His mother, a secondary wife of the Hsien Fêng Emperor, was extremely able, with towering ambition, physical vigor, and personal charm. Known best as the Empress Dowager, Tz'ŭ Hsi, or, by a familiar nickname, the Old Buddha, she was appointed co-regent with the first wife of her spouse. Until her death, in 1908, she was the chief power in the central government. She never understood the age into which the Empire was being hurried, and was superstitious, often subject to indecision, stubborn and short-sighted, but, masterful, had always to be reckoned with. A half-brother of the Hsien Fêng Emperor, best known as Prince Kung, proved to be skillful in handling relations with the Western powers. Among the Chinese officials, the ablest was Tsêng Kuo-fan, a native of Hunan, from which Mao Tse-tung and Liu Shao-Ch'i were later to come. A product of the examination system and a man of integrity, he with several other Chinese came to the support of the central government.

As a result of the efforts of this new leadership, the immediate threats to the Ch'ing were overcome and a few adjustments were made to meet the situation brought by the irruption of the West. The rebellions were suppressed. Due chiefly to the efforts of Tsêng Kuo-fan, the T'ai P'ing threat was eliminated, Nanking was taken in 1864, the initiator of the revolt committed suicide, and in the following year the remnants of the resistance were erased. In 1867 the last of the Nienfei were dispersed and in 1873 the surviving embers of the Yünnan conflagration were extinguished. Partly because of the vast distances and the desert conditions, Sinkiang was not so quickly regained, but in 1878, due largely to the remarkable achievements of Tso Tsung-t'ang, a fellow provincial of Tsêng Kuo-fan, it, too, was once more under the rule of the Ch'ing.

As an outgrowth of the near-anarchy in the neighborhood of Shanghai related to the T'ai P'ing uprising, with the consent of the Chinese officials, foreigners began the collection of the customs prescribed in the treaties. Part of the proceeds went to the payment of the indemnities incurred in the wars with the powers. From that beginning came the Imperial Maritime Customs Administration, created mainly by its second Inspector General, Robert Hart, a British subject. Under his able, selfless leadership (he held the post from 1863 to his retirement in 1907 and then was on official leave until his death in 1911) it became a striking contribution of the Westerner to the attempted adjustment of China to the contemporary world. Its top employees were foreigners among whom, by formal agreement, the British contingent outnumbered the appointees from any other country; but all employees, foreign and Chinese, were officials of the imperial government. It was established in all the treaty ports and had branch offices elsewhere. The IMCA charted the coasts and rivers, erected and maintained lighthouses, placed buoys to aid navigation, and created an empire-wide postal service. Eventually some of the domestic customs were entrusted to it. After indemnities were paid it became a useful source of revenue for Peking. In a day when corruption was rife, the Imperial Customs Administration was an example of honesty. It furthered the authority of the central government. Hart always had as his major purposes what he deemed the best interests of China, and he won the confidence of many in high command as a wise counselor.

In an attempt to deal with the new conditions in foreign relations, in 1861 the Tsungli-yamen (a special office to control foreign relations) was brought into being, its chief organizer and for many years its head, Prince Kung. The insistence of the foreign diplomats that an imperial audience be given them (on the basis of the equality guaranteed by the treaties) was granted in 1873, but still with the subtle suggestion of Chinese superiority. Chinese legations were established in Western capitals. Beginnings were made toward the creation of an army and navy equipped after the Western fashion. A few youths were sent to the United States for education.

The permeation of the Empire by Western culture slowly mounted as commerce with the Occident increased, but without much effect on the domestic scene. In the treaty ports, notably in Shanghai, communities of Westerners flourished, who under extraterritoriality were self-governing with consular cooperation, and were enclaves with a minimum of contact with the life beyond their boundaries. Roman Catholic and Protestant missionaries multiplied, especially the latter and since they were in the interior as well as the ports, they were often a target of antiforeign riots.

Here and there conflict broke out on the governmental level and a few additional encroachments were seen on Chinese sovereignty. In 1876 the Chefoo Convention with Great Britain, in settlement of an incident on the Burma frontier in which a British consular officer had been killed, safeguarded the trade across that route and opened more ports to foreign residence. In 1883 and 1884 desultory hostilities with France erupted, resulting in the recognition by China of a French protectorate over Annam and freedom of trade between Tongking and the adjacent Chinese provinces. In 1886 Great Britain annexed whatever of Burma she had not already seized, and gained recognition by Peking of the cession, but with the provision of the continuation of the decennial "tribute" missions from Burma to that capital. In 1871 Russia occupied part of Sinkiang, but after long negotiations and the threat of war by China, the Tsar's government returned part of what it had seized. In return for Portuguese cooperation in curbing the importation of opium, in 1887 Peking formally ceded to Lisbon, Macao and its dependencies—land which had long been in Portuguese hands. Further control of the opium traffic was reached through an agreement (1886) with Great Britain over the smuggling of the drug through Hong Kong. Relations with the United States were ambiguous. Friction arose over the immigration of Chinese laborers, especially to Califorina and other sections of the West Coast. Partly with the consent of China, the United States suspended the immigration for a period of years. In 1880 as part of the tentative agreement over immigration, Washington promised to forbid to American merchants and American ships participation in the importation of opium to China. In 1885 the United States returned to China the unused portion of the indemnity exacted for injuries to American merchants in Canton in 1856-1857.

The most serious of the antiforeign riots of the 1870's and 1880's were in 1870, centered in Tientsin, and were primarily directed against French Roman Catholic missionaries. Partial amends were made by the Chinese government.

Whether any viable accommodation could be achieved between the inherited culture of China and the engulfing culture of the West is debatable. For a little over three decades numbers of Chinese, Manchus, and Westerners made the attempt. By the 1890's not much alteration had been made in what had been inherited from the past; but then came a series of events which in another half century brought about an almost total change in China's civilization.

War with Japan—1894, 1895

The shock which precipitated rapid change did not come directly from the West but from a Japan which had combined much in its traditional military heritage and continental ambitions with equipment and methods derived from the West. Both tragedy and irony were seen in the fact that the blow which plunged China into revolution came from a people who owed their culture to importations from her, reshaped by their own genius. The experience was to be repeated in the 1930's and 1940's. Then, when China seemed about to have begun a successful adjustment to the Occident, she was again thrown into near chaos by attacks from Japan.

Japan had come through the nineteenth-century encounter with the West with a much more rapid accommodation than had her great neighbor. Why she had done so must be in part a subject of speculation. It may have been because she was smaller, able more quickly to communicate change to her population. The fact that in her long contacts with China she already had practice in adopting and adapting from an alien culture was probably a contributory factor. By long precedent she was military—an advantage in adjusting herself to a West in which the military tradition was a strong one. Moreover, unlike China, she had never experienced a change of dynasties. Internal strife she had frequently known, but her imperial house had been continuous from the dawn of her recorded history. Usually it had reigned but had not governed, and the actual power had been in families who successively held it in the name of the Emperor. Transition from one to another could, therefore, be accomplished with less prolonged distress than in dynastic changes in China. By professing loyalty to the Emperor, in the second half of the nineteenth century transition from feudalism to a form resembling Occidental parliamentary institutions was accomplished with relatively slight pain. Western forms of education, the beginnings of industrialization, and the construction of a navy and an army after Occidental patterns and equipped with weapons modeled on those of Europe were fairly promptly achieved.

Japanese imperialistic ambitions, a concomitant of her indigenous nationalism heightened by the contemporary example of the Occident, almost inevitably brought clashes with China. In the 1870's friction arose over the rival claims of the two empires to the Liukiu (Ryukyu) Islands but was amicably settled by the tacit relinquishment by China of her suzerainty over the disputed territory. The major conflict sprang from rivalries in Korea where China claimed suzerainty. Korea annually sent "tribute-bearing" embassies to Peking and successive Korean rulers obtained formal investiture from China, but from time immemorial the Japanese had intermittently invaded

Korea. In 1876 Japan entered into treaty relations with Korea, with the explicit recognition of the independence of that country. Even more tightly than China or Japan, Korea had kept her doors closed to the Western world. Not until the 1880's did she enter into treaty relations with Occidental powers. A struggle ensued in Seoul between the advocates of accommodation to the West and the isolationists; in general, the latter looked to China for support and the former to Japan. In 1882 a clash occurred in which the Japanese legation was attacked and both China and Japan sent troops to restore order. Two years later, in a palace upheaval, the king sought refuge with the Japanese guard, the Japanese occupied the palace, and Chinese troops joined in an assault on the Japanese. In 1885 both Japan and China agreed to evacuate their troops from Korea, not to send them again without notifying the other, and to withdraw them as soon as order was restored. China sought to strengthen her hold on the country. Early in the 1890's a rebellion broke out in Korea which Korean forces suppressed, but China, at the request of Seoul, sent forces and the Japanese did likewise.

War followed between China and Japan (1894-1895), and despite heroic resistance, the Chinese were promptly defeated on both sea and land; Port Arthur and Weihaiwei, the one on the Liaotung Peninsula jutting southward from Manchuria and the other opposite to it in the Shantung peninsula and both fortified after Western methods, fell to the Japanese. Part of the reason for the debacle was corruption in high quarters. For example, in her semiretirement the Empress Dowager diverted some of the funds allocated to the building of a navy on Western models and used them for the construction of an elaborate summer palace northwest of Peking.

In the ensuing Peace Treaty of Shimonoseki (1895), China acknowledged the independence of Korea, and ceded to Japan, Formosa, the Pescadores Islands, and the Liaotung Peninsula, paid an indemnity, opened four more ports, and granted most favored nation treatment. In the treaty of commerce which followed, Japan was given extraterritorial status.

European Aggression

The defeat of China by Japan precipitated a series of aggressions by European powers which threatened the dismemberment of the Empire. The closing years of the nineteenth century were marked by the climax of Western imperialism in Africa, in most of Asia except China, Japan, and Siam (Thailand), in the remnants of the Turkish

Empire, called significantly "the sick man of Europe," and in most of Arabia. Such lands of difficult terrain as Afghanistan were subject to the West, or, as in the case of Persia (Iran), were about to be carved into spheres of influence. All the islands of the Pacific except Hawaii and part of Samoa were in possession of European governments, and Hawaii was clearly soon to be annexed by the United States and part of Samoa was in its possession.

The aggressions can be quickly summarized. Because of a French, Russian, and German protest, Japan renounced her claim to the Liaotung Peninsula in return for an increased indemnity. Bankers of the rival powers contended for the monopoly of lending to China the sums to pay the indemnity—on the security of the customs revenue, the salt tax, and some of the internal transit tax. In 1895 China agreed to a French request for a sphere of interest in the three southwest provinces, Yünnan, Kwangsi, and Kwangtung, which bordered on Annam, at that time a French protectorate. This entailed, among other concessions, permission to build railways and the employment of French experts in the development of these areas. Alarmed by the threat to Burma, in 1897 Great Britain obtained privileges in the area immediately north of that country. In 1898 Germany was granted a ninety-nine-year lease of Kiaochow Bay, a harbor which commanded the southern part of Shantung. That same year Russia acquired a twenty-five-year lease on Talienwan (also known as Dalney and Dairen), a port commanding the entrance to Manchuria, and on Port Arthur, the fortified post on the Liaotung Peninsula. Thus Russia was assured control of all Manchuria. To counter the Russian move and to safeguard her interests in North China, in 1898 Great Britain obtained a lease on Weihaiwei, a stronghold on the northern coast of Shantung and nearly opposite Port Arthur, "for so long a period as Port Arthur shall remain in the possession of Russia." She also was given a ninety-nine-year lease on that part of Kowloon, the New Territories, opposite Hong Kong, which had not been ceded to her in 1860. In 1898 she asked and was promised that China would not alienate to a third power any territory in the provinces in the Yangtze Valley since her commercial interests were centered there. In 1897 France was formally assured that China would not cede the island of Hainan to a third power, and the following year France was given a ninety-nine-year lease on Kwangchowwan, a bay in Kwangtung, and a commitment for the provinces bordering her territories in Indo-China similar to that which had been given her for Hainan. The powers engaged in competition for the construction of railways in China, the Russians obtaining a grant for rail lines in Manchuria which further strengthened their hold on that vast area, the French, English, and Germans acquiring similar grants in areas which they regarded as their spheres of interest.

To counter these preliminaries to the partition of China, in 1899 the United States put forward what became known as "the open door policy." The United States had not joined in the scramble for China, but by its annexation of the Philippines and of Hawaii in 1898 it had moved into and across the Pacific. It now sent notes to Japan and the European powers most involved, asking that in their respective spheres of interest Chinese administration would be respected in the collection of customs duties, that harbor dues and railroad charges would be the same for the citizens of every nation, and that existing interests of all nations would be free from interference. The request was designed to conserve the commercial and financial interests of Americans, but it also had the disinterested purpose of safeguarding what came to be called "the independence and territorial integrity" of China. It became the cornerstone of American Chinese policy and was increasingly to involve the United States in China and East Asia.

Chinese Reformers Try to Save Their Country

To many Chinese the defeat by Japan and the threatened partition of the Empire came as a shock which impelled them to efforts to save their country by more thoroughgoing measures than had been adopted in the preceding three decades. Numerous reform societies sprang up, among them some sponsored by outstanding products of the Confucian system. Several foreigners, notably the Welsh Protestant missionary, Timothy Richards, endeavored to help by producing literature to acquaint Chinese with the Occident and by suggesting concrete measures. A number of Chinese who were not in official posts were vocal and won the ear of the Kuang Hsü Emperor, who, then in his late twenties, had been put on the throne by the Empress Dowager in 1875, as an infant, and had been kept under her dominance. Intelligent, he owed to a tutor instruction in English and some acquaintance with world affairs. In 1898, following the advice of some of the advocates of change, in what came to be known as the "hundred days' reform," the Kuang Hsü Emperor issued a succession of decrees which, if carried out, would have worked important adjustments to the new age. Judged by what was later accomplished they were relatively mild.

Violent Reaction and Further Humiliation

However, the reaction against reform was prompt and, before long, violent. The Empress Dowager, Tz'ŭ Hsi, distrusted the independence shown by one who owed his position to her. Around her were many whose livelihoods were threatened by the innovations. The Emperor's advisors plotted to eliminate the leading conservatives and to deprive the Empress Dowager of her power, but she acted promptly. She had the Emperor confined to a pavilion in the palace and compelled him to cancel his reform decrees and to request her to resume control of the government. He was able to warn one of his advisers in time for him to escape. Several others were punished and at least six were executed.

At first, independent of support by the Empress Dowager, an uprising broke out which had as its objective the expulsion or death of the foreigners—blamed as they were for the Empire's misfortunes. It was headed by groups known to foreigners as the Boxers—partly from their Chinese name and partly from their gymnastic exercises—and activities were mostly in the North. By 1899 they were annoying foreigners and in 1900 they killed a number, chiefly missionaries who by the nature of their work were often remote from the Western-defended treaty ports. Thousands of Chinese Christians, who had accepted the foreign-sponsored religion, were also killed. In the summer of that year Boxers besieged the foreigners and Chinese Christians who had taken refuge in the legation quarter in Peking and the Chinese Christians who had sought haven in the Roman Catholic cathedral in that city. To protect their nationals, the powers assembled an allied force in Tientsin which within a few weeks fought its way to Peking and relieved the beleaguered. The Empress Dowager fled, taking the Emperor with her. Due partly to the efforts of viceroys and governors in the Yangtze Valley and Canton, the powers did not consider themselves at war with China, but as merely suppressing local uprisings which were imperiling their nationals.

Although no formal state of war had existed, for over a decade after 1900 China was in fact a foreign-occupied country. After much wrangling among themselves and long negotiations with the Chinese, the powers imposed on China what was known as the Boxer Protocol. Among its several provisions the Protocol levied on China a large indemnity to compensate for the damage done to foreigners and to help defray the expenses of the allied forces; provided for the stationing of foreign troops in Peking to protect the legations in that city; agreed to the razing of the forts which commanded the entrance to Tientsin and thus to the approach from the sea to Peking; gave assurance of free access to Peking by stationing foreign troops at strategic points between that city and Tientsin; and promised the reconstruction of the Tsungli-Yamen into a Ministry of Foreign Affairs which would have precedent over all the other ministries of state—thus according a dignity to relations with other governments which would once for all acknowledge to the world that other nations were on an equality with China and not, as the Chinese had traditionally considered axiomatic, subordinate to the Middle Kingdom.

The Russo-Japanese War

Further humiliation soon came to the Chinese in a war between Russia and Japan (1904-1905). Using as an excuse the threat to her interests by the Boxer uprising, Russia had moved troops into Manchuria. After peace had been restored, in spite of repeated promises to evacuate her forces, she continued her occupation and appeared to be intent on making it a prelude to annexation. Reinforced by a treaty of alliance with Great Britain (formed in 1902), Japan suddenly struck. Her primary concern was Korea, for Russia was seeking to extend her tentacles over that country, where, after her war with China in the preceding decade, Japan was strengthening her hold. But the ambitions of the island empire were already wider. The fighting was chiefly in Manchuria, on Chinese soil, with the Ch'ing having to be a helpless, officially neutral spectator. Japan won and took over the Russian railroads and leaseholds in the southern portion of that potentially rich but undeveloped region. The way was thus prepared for her later fateful adventures in China.

FOUR

REVOLUTIONARY TRANSITIONS

The Boxer year and its aftermath were a bitter experience for the Chinese. Their pride was still unbroken, but it smarted under the humiliation of the foreign invasion and the Protocol, adding as it did to the existing restrictions on the Empire's sovereignty. They were further outraged by the Empire's helplessness in the face of the Russo-Japanese War.

Now began earnest attempts to adjust to the world which had so rudely thrust itself on the country. Because of inexperience many were ill-conceived and imperfectly carried out, but all contributed to the changes that occurred in the twentieth century.

The Ch'ing rulers sought to lead. The Empress Dowager, now back in Peking from her haven in Sian (the former Ch'angan), discerned, but still dimly, the writing on the wall, and she had many of the reforms put into force which the Kuang Hsü Emperor had decreed but which she had canceled. In 1905 an imperial edict was issued which abolished the civil service examinations and ordered that a system of new tests for public office be substituted, based on Western as well as Chinese subjects. Thus, by one stroke of the vermilion pencil, the method which dated from the Han dynasty for recruiting civil officials was erased and with it went the foundation of the time-honored education based on Confucianism which itself was irreparably weakened. Within a generation the majority of Chinese youth would have at best only a nodding acquaintance with its classical books and one of the chief supports of China's traditional culture had been removed. The Ch'ing also instituted measures to frame a constitution on Western models, with representative assemblies chosen by popular election.

In other ways, apart from the Ch'ing, attempts were made to adjust to the new day. Provincial and local officials and some private individuals set up schools in which Western subjects constituted the major part of the curriculum. But they were handicapped by the lack of adequate physical equipment and trained teachers. Christian missionaries, notably Protestants, by selfless service, opened and maintained schools, hospitals, and dispensaries, in which Western learning and methods were employed. Chinese youth, at first a bare trickle which soon swelled to a flood, went abroad to acquire foreign learning, the majority seeking it in Japan as the nearest and least expensive source, but many in Europe and especially the United States. Railways were put through, largely with foreign capital and on foreign initiative. Factories were constructed, chiefly for textiles; iron works were erected; and mines were developed, also mainly by foreigners. After their acquisition of the Russian holdings in Southern Manchuria, the Japanese undertook the exploitation of the mineral resources of the region.

A Perilous Experiment with a Republic

For the Ch'ing dynasty the sands were rapidly running out. In 1908 the Empress Dowager breathed her last and within a few hours the Kuang Hsü Emperor joined her in the land of the shades. One of the last acts of the Empress Dowager was the appointment of an infant, Pu-i, to succeed the Kuang Hsü Emperor; the reign title was Hsüan T'ung. Neither the regent nor any others close to the throne had the ability required by the national crisis.

What would follow, no one could accurately predict. Heretofore, as the imperial line, recruited by heredity, declined in vigor, the end of a dynasty had been presaged by revolts. After a longer or shorter period of civil strife either the leader of one of the revolts or a foreign invader had seized the throne. The realistically minded Chinese would see in this denouement the transfer of the mandate of Heaven. However, the new currents entering from abroad and the rival imperialisms of Western powers made impossible the repetition of the traditional transition. Some of the more radical reformers were dreaming of China as a republic.

In October, 1911, a revolt broke out among the troops at Wuchang —one of the three cities which constituted the Wuhan center at a strategic point on the Yangtze, the other two being Hankow and

Hanyang. October 10—"the Double Tenth"—became the date celebrated by the Republic of China. A republic was declared and all three cities quickly were controlled by the rebels.

To meet the emergency Peking called on Yüan Shih-kai. Yüan Shih-kai was in command of the strongest army in China, one which was equipped with Western weapons. Although within a few weeks Hankow was retaken, the rebellion had spread like wildfire. City after city and province after province declared its independence of the Ch'ing dynasty and set up a provisional government. The Manchu garrisons placed in strategic cities at the time of the founding of the Ch'ing had become flabby; their helpless members were massacred. Before the end of 1911 representatives of the various local and provincial bodies had gathered in Nanking as a national council and elected Sun Yat-sen as president of the republic.

Sun Yat-sen had long been a revolutionary. Born in 1866 in a village near Canton, he was the son of a tenant-farmer. When he was in his early teens an older brother who had emigrated to Hawaii paid his expenses to those islands and put him in a school in Honolulu conducted by an Anglican bishop, where he became convinced of the truth of the faith taught by the bishop. His brother, alarmed, had him sent back to China, but the lad, true to his new convictions, disfigured the images in the local temple, and for this sacrilege had to flee. He found haven in Canton and was befriended by a Protestant missionary. He was next in Hong Kong where he studied medicine, was baptized, and given a medical diploma (1892). He began practicing his profession in Macao. He had become an ardent reformer and gathered about him a group made up chiefly of former students in Protestant mission schools. Since Peking did not heed his petition to start an agricultural college, he joined in a plot against the Manchus. The plot was discovered and he took refuge in Hong Kong (1895) and then in Japan. For most of the time between 1895 and 1911 he traveled extensively among the overseas Chinese, seeking to enlist them against the Manchus and in support of a republic. He read prodigiously and worked out a program for the republic. He was a visionary, an agitator, and not an administrator or an executive. The fame he had acquired in his years of wandering led many who were looking for a leader in the adventure of the republic to regard him as their best hope.

Sober minds perceived that the country had everything to lose if it engaged in prolonged civil strife. Chaos would follow, and foreign powers might step in and complete the dismemberment of the Empire. Even before Sun Yat-sen reached Nanking, negotiations had begun. Yüan Shih-kai succeeded in convincing the court that it must yield to the inevitable. On February 12, 1912, edicts were issued in the name of the child Emperor in which he abdicated and entrusted to Yüan Shih-kai the organization of a republic. The terms of the abdication were generous: Pu-i was to retain for life the title of Emperor, was to be granted a large annuity, and was to have the use of a palace.

So perished the imperial institution through which China had been ruled for more than two thousand years. The Confucian monarchy had been abolished; another basic stone in the foundation of the traditional culture disappeared. The chief remaining bulwark of the Confucian order was the family, but the historic order was rapidly crumbling.

The Stormy First Years

For several years the Chinese floundered about in their attempt to achieve a viable republican form of government with the result that in a little over a decade, as could be expected, a central government commanding the allegiance of the country had almost disappeared. The failure arose from lack of experience rather than basic inability, for the Chinese had long demonstrated their political competence. Although far from faultless, the government developed in China over the centuries had been as nearly successful in maintaining internal order, in facilitating a livelihood for the masses, and in freeing the human spirit for cultural creativity as any other in the previous record of mankind. But the Chinese had never known a republic or republican institutions. Nor were they prepared for a representative democracy as the Anglo-Saxon world understood that word. Over many centuries Anglo-Saxons had only painfully and imperfectly approached that ideal and, outside the British Empire and the United States, Western Europeans in general were still groping their way toward that goal. Decades of suffering lay ahead of the Chinese before they could achieve forms of government which would approach the record of the Confucian monarchy—which, perforce, they had thrown into the dustbin.

The most promising course for avoiding chaos was adopted. Sun Yat-sen resigned the presidency and Yüan Shih-kai was elected to fill the post. Li Yüan-hung, who had led the revolt in Wuchang, was chosen vice-president. Thus the new government was assured military support. Manchus, Tibetans, Mongols, and Moslems—the major minority peoples—were promised equality with the Han Chinese and security in their titles and property. Recognition was granted by foreign powers, and for a few months some prospect was seen that internal order would be restored and preserved.

The hope of peaceful transition from a monarchy to a republic proved illusory, however. Yüan Shih-kai soon clashed with parliament and some of the military in the South. Parliament had a large majority of radicals and attempted to make the president a figurehead, somewhat like what was then true of the Third Republic of France. Yüan would not consent and showed his independence by negotiating, without parliamentary consent, a loan from foreign bankers needed to tide over his regime until internal revenues ample for his needs were assured. He attempted to supplant military commanders in the Yangtze Valley and the South with men he could trust. Revolt broke out, and with the endorsement of Sun Yat-sen a "punitive expedition" sought to unseat Yüan. Yüan quickly suppressed it and Sun Yat-sen fled to Japan. Yüan purged parliament of his opponents in November, 1913, and dismissed the remnant of that body in January, 1914. In 1915 he announced the restoration of the monarchy with himself the first Emperor of a new dynasty. When opposition broke into open rebellion, Yüan first postponed his formal enthronement and then canceled the monarchy. His opponents, unappeased, pressed their attack. In June, 1916, ill and humiliated by his loss of face, Yüan Shih-kai died.

An effort to bring all the factions into the government soon broke down. Li Yüan-hung was moved up into the presidency, with a warlord, Fêng Kuo-chang, who had come to prominence in the Yangtze Valley, as vice-president, the parliament dismissed by Yüan was recalled, and Tuan Ch'i-jui, who headed the military clique that ruled the army gathered by Yüan Shih-kai, was retained as premier, the office to which the latter had appointed him.

The inevitable dissension was precipitated by the decision to enter World War I; in March, 1917, China broke off relations with Germany, and Tuan wished China to take the next step and declare war. Parliament, controlled by the elements that had broken with Yüan Shih-kai, refused to concur unless Tuan was dismissed to which Li Yüan-hung complied. The military who supported Tuan declared the independence of several provinces in the North, where Yüan Shih-kai had had his strength and of which they were heirs. Chang Hsün, a warlord who controlled the railway line from Tientsin to the Yangtze, induced Li Yüan-hung to dismiss parliament. He then came to

Peking and, in July, 1917, declaring the Ch'ing dynasty restored, placed the boy Emperor, Pu-i, again on the throne. Within a few days the northern generals (generally known by the title of *tuchun*), unwilling to see Chang Hsün in control, marched on Peking, took it, retired Pu-i, and declared the republic restored. Chang Hsün sought haven in the Dutch legation. Li Yüan-hung, having suffered great loss of face, refused to resume the presidency and lived comfortably in the security of the foreign concessions in Tientsin. Tuan was again premier, and the military clique of which he was a member, usually called the Anfu Club, placed in the presidency Hsü Shih-ch'ang, an elderly ex-official of the Ch'ing. The dissident members of the parliament of 1913 assembled in Shanghai and Canton and set up a regime, usually with headquarters in the latter city, which they declared to be the only legitimate government of the country. In 1921 it elected Sun Yat-sen as president, but its hold, even in the South, was precarious.

While China was in the throes of transition from the Confucian monarchy to the initial experiment with a republic, the outlying dependencies of Outer Mongolia and Tibet which had been brought within the Empire by the Manchus were slipping away and further humiliation was suffered because of Japanese aggression.

Late in 1911 leaders in Outer Mongolia took the occasion of the weakness of the Ch'ing to declare independence, and the leading Buddhist monk was made the head of state. The next year Russia recognized the autonomy of the region. In 1913 Peking assented to that status in return for Russian acknowledgment of China's suzerainty over the region. In 1915 Russia, China, and Outer Mongolia entered into an agreement confirming that arrangement. The ground was thus laid for further rivalry of Russia and China in Outer Mongolia and the Russian gain when, in 1961, the U.S.S.R. obtained the recognition by the United Nations of the independence of the country and its membership in that body.

In Tibet, British and Russian rivalries were chronic. Great Britain was fearful of the growth of the Tsar's power on the northern frontiers of India, then a part of Britain's empire. In 1906 the English, to strengthen what they declared to be their interests in Tibet, dispatched an expedition which took Lhasa, the capital of Tibet. The English then exacted a treaty which made Tibet more accessible to their trade by way of India, placing that country within the British sphere of influence by the device, familiar in recent Chinese history, of a promise by the Tibetans that they would not cede or lease any of their territory to any foreign power. The Dalai Lama had taken refuge with fellow Buddhists in Mongolia. In 1907 Great Britain and Russia recognized the suzerainty of China over Tibet. In 1910 a Chinese army fought its way through to Lhasa, and the Dalai Lama, now back in that city, fled to Darjeeling, in India. At that time, the English warned China that they would not permit interference in the border states—Nepal, Sikkim, and Bhutan. In 1911 the Tibetans, taking advantage of the civil strife in China, drove the Chinese troops out of most of the country and the Dalai Lama returned to Lhasa. In 1913-1914 England, China, and Tibet signed a convention by which China's sovereignty was recognized, but Peking agreed not to convert the region into a province. A dividing line known as the MacMahon line (from the name of the British representative) defined the boundary between Tibet and the British possessions and dependencies on the mountainous border. However, as we have seen, China would not agree to the MacMahon line but insisted on a boundary which would include all the territory occupied by her troops. Friendliness between Great Britain and Tibet increased and in 1922, at the request of the Tibetans, Lhasa was linked by telegraph to India. In its Tibetan policy in the 1950's and 1960's and in its undeclared war with India the People's Republic of China was holding to the claims of both the Ch'ing and the Republic of China.

Fresh Japanese aggression accompanied World War I. While Europe was preoccupied with that struggle, Japan took the opportunity to extend her control in China. In 1914, giving as a reason her alliance with Great Britain, Japan took possession of Kiaochow, the German leasehold on the coast of Shantung. In January, 1915, she followed this up with what were known as the Twenty-one Demands, which if granted, would have made all China a sphere of influence of her island neighbor, thus extending Japanese control over much of its life. Peking demurred, but after months of negotiations acceded to the less sweeping of the demands.

China in World War I and Its Aftermath

In spite of the internal division precipitated by the question of entry into World War I, in August, 1917, the regime centered in Peking declared war on the Central Powers. Since that was the government accredited by the outer world, China was formally recognized as a belligerent.

From the standpoint of China the result of this act was ambiguous. On the one hand it strengthened Japan's hold. China and Japan entered into agreements for cooperation in naval and military activities, a "war participation board" was set up with a Japanese adviser, an "arms contract" was entered into between Peking and Tokyo, and the latter made extensive loans to the former on the security of railways, mines, forests, telegraphs, and taxes. On the other hand China canceled the German concessions in Tientsin and Hankow and the Austro-Hungarian concession in Tientsin. She also obtained a seat in the peace conference in Paris.

At the peace conference China was represented by both the Peking and Canton regimes. She failed to prevent the transfer to Japan of the German holdings in Shantung, but Japan promised eventually to restore them to her. She declined to sign the general treaty with Germany and concluded a separate treaty with that late enemy. However, she obtained membership in the League of Nations by subscribing to the general treaty with Austria. Both Germany and Austria lost their extraterritorial status, their special concessions, and their share in the Boxer indemnity. Thus a breach was made in the wall of foreign privileges in China.

In the years immediately following World War I, China made further gains in canceling her subservience to foreign powers. The tide of revolt against European domination in Asia and Africa which rose to a flood after World War II was already beginning. The Chinese took advantage of it. As in many other parts of the world, nationalism was a growing force. In spite of their interior divisions and inability to make their will effective by armed force, the Chinese profited by European weakness, presented their case to the world, and through boycotts against foreigners and foreign trade made substantial advances.

In 1921-1922 an international conference was held in Washington on the limitation of armaments and on Pacific and Far Eastern questions. Its purpose was to ease rising tensions and an incipient naval arms race. The tensions had arisen especially from American opposition to Japanese ambitions in China and restrictions on Japanese immigration to the United States. As an outcome, curbs were placed on naval competition in the Pacific. By the "Nine Power Treaty" all participants in the conference promised to respect the sovereignty, the independence, and the territorial integrity of China, to refrain from taking advantage of conditions in China to seek special privileges, and to give the Chinese an opportunity to achieve a stable government. They agreed to a revision of the customs duties and to a study of extraterritoriality with a view to its eventual abolishment.

The withdrawal of foreign postal agencies was promised. The Chinese and Japanese used the opportunity to reach an agreement on controversial issues. Japan withdrew in part from her special position in Shantung and gave assurances that she would not press some of the concessions obtained through the Twenty-one Demands. Great Britain promised to restore Weihaiwei to China.

The Russian Revolution of 1917 which brought the Communists to power and established the U.S.S.R. gave the Chinese an opportunity to regain some of the ground which they had lost to the Tsarist regime. For a little over a year in 1919-1921 they re-established their authority in Outer Mongolia. In 1924 an agreement was reached through which Russian extraterritorial privileges were relinquished, the Russian portion of the Boxer indemnity was canceled, and some hope was held out that the Chinese would gain control of the Russian portion of the Manchurian railways. In 1929 the Chinese seized full control of these railways, but the Russians brought in troops and forced the Chinese to consent to the joint operation of the lines which had previously been the agreed arrangement.

Agitation and boycotts increased against the foreign concessions in the treaty ports which were really foreign enclaves. They were under the resident consuls and some were controlled by councils elected by the foreign taxpayers. To the Chinese Shanghai was especially irritating as the port with the largest foreign trade and the major center of foreign banking. There the International Settlement and the French Concession had most of the foreign residences and business. In Shanghai the Mixed Court in which Chinese defendants were tried had been taken over by the consular body at the time of the revolution of 1911. On May 30, 1925, disturbances in connection with a strike led the foreign police, goaded to self-defense by Communist agitators, to fire into the crowd. An anti-foreign, chiefly anti-British, explosion followed, and the resulting boycott lasted for months and cost British merchants millions of dollars. The May 30 incident became a landmark in anti-foreign nationalism. On June 23, 1925, an armed clash broke out against the foreign settlement in Canton, and in 1927 the British concessions in Hankow and Kiukiang were seized. In that year the Mixed Court in Shanghai was restored to the Chinese and Chinese were admitted to membership in the councils which governed the concessions in that port. By 1931 several other concessions had been turned over to the Chinese and nearly all the powers, with the notable exception of Japan, had consented to the full control of the tariffs by the Chinese. The Customs

Service was more and more under Chinese administration. The Chinese were persistent in seeking to end extraterritoriality and what they called the "unequal treaties," and before 1930 over half the foreigners in China no longer had extraterritorial privileges; only the United States, Japan, Great Britain, and France held out for the continuation of that status for their citizens. The Chinese were increasingly restive under the Japanese control of South Manchuria, for they were moving into the region by the tens of thousands and for a time the largest migration on the globe was said to be by the Chinese into what had been a thinly populated area which the Manchus had vainly attempted to keep as their special preserve.

The agitation for the removal of the foreign restrictions on national sovereignty arose chiefly from the resentment of a proud people who had long been accustomed to regarding their land—"the Middle Kingdom"—as the center of civilized man, which conferred titles on rulers of other nations, and which received tribute in recognition of its superiority. The Chinese had felt outraged and humiliated by the concessions which they had been forced to grant in the preceding eight or nine decades. The intellectuals, and especially the students, were particularly vocal and insistent. The Communists took advantage of the situation to enhance their influence and in 1949, when they came to power, they continued to appeal to the intense nationalism which had roots in traditional Chinese convictions.

Intellectual Life

The end of the traditional examination system and the influx of Western thought by way of modern schools and students returning from Japan, Europe and America brought an intellectual revolution which found expression in a variety of ways. At one of its peaks, reached in the 1920's, it was called the "New Tide," or the Renaissance, and was fed by the new schools which were springing into existence. The new scholar class in 1919, through the May Fourth Movement, attempted to lead in the cultural and political revolution and for a time appeared to succeed.

With their traditional confidence in education, the Chinese were seeking both to prepare an elite comparable to the old scholar class and to make the masses literate and equipped with the knowledge essential to life in the age into which the nation was being thrust. Elementary, secondary, and higher schools multiplied, though the physical equipment and the thousands of teachers required could not be immediately obtained and much of the education was inferior.

REVOLUTIONARY TRANSITIONS

Moreover, students were restive. They participated in the boycotts and the agitation against foreign privileges and resented efforts of the authorities at intellectual discipline. Yet some institutions succeeded in attaining high standards. A flood of books and periodicals issued from the presses. Philosophies handed down from the past were challenged and ancient philosophies long ignored were re-examined. Western philosophical systems were studied. Some contemporary philosophers, among them John Dewey and Bertrand Russell, were popular.

A major change was the shift from the classical style of written Chinese to a dignified form of the vernacular. In this field, Hu Shih (1891-1962) was an outstanding leader. As a youth he had been trained in the traditional learning, then had been a student in the United States at Cornell and Columbia, and had been especially impressed by John Dewey. He was one of the brilliant coterie that in the 1920's made the National University in Peking the chief radiating center of the New Tide. Many writers of fiction emerged, some of them widely read.

Several of the short stories and novels of the New Tide dealt with relations between the sexes and the family. They were very critical of the traditional family system and the custom of having marriages arranged by the elders without the consent of the couple. This trend indicated the beginning of the disintegration of the kind of family pattern associated with Confucianism and thus the crumbling of another bulwark of the Confucian culture.

A phase of the intellectual nationalist ferment was an anti-religious, mainly anti-Christian movement which denounced Christianity as obscurantist intellectually and as allied with Western imperialism. It particularly opposed the control by foreigners of the schools under missionary auspices and demanded that in them attendance at religious services and religious instruction be voluntary and that the heads of schools be Chinese.

At the same time something of a revival was seen in non-Christian religions. New syncretic cults appeared. An awakening occurred in Buddhism with an attempt to give instruction to the laity.

The changes in the intellectual life which we noted in our first chapter and which characterized the China of the People's Republic had begun before the triumph of that regime. Here as in so much else of their program the Communists carried through in more drastic fashion the revolution which had begun to take form before they came to power. In their atheism and their insistence that the churches sever all ties with Christians outside China they were carrying further the antireligious, anti-Christian movement of the 1920's.

The developing revolution in the social patterns of China's life was closely related to that in the intellectual life of the country, for it was most marked among the students and the younger intelligentsia. More and more the young were arranging their own marriages, increasingly women were being educated in the same schools with men and were in occupations previously reserved for men, and the old forms of courtesy were passing. Here, too, the communists later accelerated what had begun.

Toward Political Unity

By a strange contrast, some of the gains against foreign privileges were achieved when internal national political union had reached its nadir. Attempts were made to reverse the disintegration. Several warlords entered into kaleidoscopic coalitions which disintegrated almost as quickly as they were formed. Attempts were made to draw up what were euphemistically declared to be permanent constitutions, but which proved to be ephemeral. In 1926 only a semblance of a national government remained in Peking—it did not have a president and even the post of "provisional chief executive" was vacant. Recurring civil strife among the rival military figures was almost as regular as the arrival of spring and summer. The nation was weary of the fighting and was willing to welcome any leadership which seemed to hold promise of domestic peace and order.

In 1926 that leadership was appearing in a revived and reorganized Kuomintang or Nationalist Party. Sun Yat-sen, its central figure, died (of cancer) in Peking on March 12, 1925, during a conference with two of the more prominent warlords in an effort to restore domestic peace. Two years earlier he had called to his assistance Russian Communists, and with their advice had reshaped the Kuomintang on the pattern of the Russian Communist Party, but he did not adopt the Communist ideology. Instead, he left behind him a last will and testament directed to the nation and several books which outlined his program. Of the latter, the one which became most influential was the *San Min Chu I*, "the Three People's Principles." The three principles were government of the people, by the people, and for the people; a sufficient livelihood for all; and freedom from foreign control. The Kuomintang proclaimed Sun Yat-sen to be the national hero and professed to adopt his program. The Communists sought to infiltrate the Kuomintang: through their incentive, unions were organized of peasants and laborers which were directed against landlords and foreigners.

In the summer of 1926 the armies of the Kuomintang began a northward march, presumably to attempt establishment of a national government. The armies were staffed by officers trained in a special school in Canton, and at their head was Chiang Kai-shek (1887-   ). In his training Chiang Kai-shek, with part of his education in Japan, was a product of the old China and the new forces. The Kuomintang armies faced little opposition south of the Yangtze; early in the spring of 1927 they reached that river and such strategic centers as Wuchang, Hankow, and Shanghai were occupied.

Further advance was temporarily halted by dissensions within the Kuomintang between the Communists and the moderates. The Communist elements, who were vigorously anti-imperialist and anti-foreign, wished to dispossess landlords and made drastic demands of foreigners. Blatantly anti-Christian, they labeled Chinese Christians "the running dogs" of the foreigners. In March, 1927, radical elements in the army roughly handled foreigners in Nanking and the more extreme Communists organized a government with headquarters in Hankow.

By the close of 1927 public opinion had turned overwhelmingly against the Communists, and the moderates, under Chiang Kai-shek, were in control. The government in Hankow had been terminated, the Russian advisers had taken flight, many of the radicals had been executed, and others, including the American-educated widow of Sun Yat-sen, were in exile. Chiang Kai-shek strengthened his position by his marriage to a sister of Sun Yat-sen's widow. She, too, was American-educated—as was her brother, T. V. Soong. She was a Christian, a Methodist. The marriage was a Christian ceremony and before long Chiang Kai-shek was baptized, also as a Methodist. His move to Christianity was yet another and personal reason for opposition to atheistic communism.

In 1928 the armies of the Kuomintang, no longer weakened by internal divisions, resumed their northward march and in June of that year entered Peking. Their most formidable opponent was Chang Tso-lin, an able and ruthless warlord, who had ruled Manchuria since the early days of the republic. While retreating from Peking to Mukden, his capital, he was killed by a bomb, presumably dropped on his train by Japanese. His son and heir, Chang Hsüeh-liang (1898-   ), made his peace with the Kuomintang and accepted a post in its organization. We have already met him in the dramatic incident of 1936.

Not all the country submitted to the Kuomintang. Here and there were recalcitrant warlords and some of their number who cooperated with the Kuomintang maintained a semi-independence. Remnants of the Communists rallied, but without Russian advisers, and before long set up a government south of the Yangtze. As we have seen, they there adopted vigorous methods against the landlords, and soon Mao Tse-tung emerged as their leader.

The Kuomintang and the Prospect of Progress

For a few years after 1928 the prospect for internal unity and recovery from the long years of domestic strife appeared to have high promise. The capital was established at Nanking, and Peking was renamed Peiping ("Northern Peace"). In Nanking new government buildings appeared, the body of Sun Yat-sen was brought with great ceremony to that city and a monumental tomb was erected for it in semi-Western, semi-Chinese style—a symbol of the harmonious fusion of the new with the old which it was hoped would characterize the future. The government enlisted the support of many of the younger generation with training in the West or on Western patterns. Sympathetic foreign residents and observers thought that they saw indications that China's long agony and weakness were passing and that the Chinese would make a successful and creative adjustment to the modern world. Here and there were inefficiency and corruption, but they were no more pronounced than in some of the greatest periods in China's history or than in many strong Western governments. Education was being improved and extended to a growing proportion of the population, cities were being modernized, automobiles and airplanes were improving communication, railroads were being repaired after the damage wrought by the years of domestic war, banditry was being reduced, and progress was being made in regaining the nation's full autonomy. Many observers held that had Japan not intruded into the domestic scene the Kuomintang would have succeeded in effecting an orderly transition to a China which would have had much of what the Anglo-Saxon world called democracy. That, however, was not to be.

The Japanese Invasion

The hopeful years were halted by Japanese attempts to dominate the country and to set up regimes which would cooperate with them.

The first dramatic move was in Manchuria in September, 1931. Ever since she had displaced Russia in South Manchuria in 1905, Japan had been developing the rich resources of that region with coal mines, steel works, and other industrial plants. Japan needed raw materials, especially iron, which were not in sufficient quantity in the homeland, and she wanted markets for the products of her factories. The vast, relatively undeveloped resources and potential markets of China in general and Manchuria in particular seemed to be exactly what was required. Chinese patriots, however, resented what they regarded as Japanese intrusion on their nation's soil as an obstacle to their program to regain their country's full autonomy. Chang Hsüeh-liang and his government frequently annoyed the Japanese. Moreover, the Chinese were deliberately projecting railway lines which would seriously compete with the Japanese rail system in South Manchuria. To the irritation of Chinese nationalists, Koreans who were at that time Japanese subjects were moving by the thousand from their overcrowded peninsula into the relatively vacant lands to the west of the Yalu.

Suddenly and without warning, the Japanese sought to cut the Gordian knot. On the night of September 18-19, 1931, Japanese troops seized Mukden and within the next few weeks took possession of several other strategic centers, both in their own sphere and in the Russian sphere in North Manchuria. Since most of Chang Hsüeh-liang's forces were south of the Great Wall with headquarters in Peiping, he was powerless to check the Japanese. Early in 1932, the Japanese set up, ostensibly on the initiative of Chinese and Mongols, a state called Manchukuo, which was declared independent of China, and had as its head Pu-i, the last Ch'ing Emperor. Later in that year Japan officially recognized Manchukuo and concluded with it a defensive alliance, but Manchukuo and Pu-i were puppets and were controlled by Japanese advisers.

All this was accomplished in defiance of the League of Nations. Promptly after the Mukden incident China appealed to that body and a League of Nations commission was appointed to study the situation. The report of the commission satisfied neither Japan nor China: in February, 1933, the Assembly of the League condemned Japan, and within a few days Japan withdrew her membership from the League. Although not a member of the League, the United States early expressed its hope that both Japan and China would refrain from hostilities.

Japan, not content with Manchuria, aspired to the control of

Inner Mongolia and the northern portions of China proper. In 1933 China and Japan arrived at a truce by which the former agreed to remove her troops from an area between Peking and the Great Wall and the former was to retire its armies to the north of that barrier. After 1933 the Japanese army moved westward into Inner Mongolia and the northeastern provinces of China proper. A year later, Pu-i was given the title of Emperor. That year Japan warned the world that she would not permit in China financial aid or military advisers from another country and thus in effect sought to make China her protectorate. In 1935, in seeming acquiescence, the U.S.S.R. sold to Japan its holdings in her railways in Manchuria. In 1935 the Japanese constrained the Chinese to withdraw part of their forces from Hopei, the province in which Peiping was situated. The same year a rumor spread that the Japanese were about to set up an "autonomous" region embracing much of the Northeast and independent of Nanking.

As a phase of China's resistance to Japan, in 1936, as we have mentioned, an uneasy truce was made between the Communists and the Kuomintang. The preceding year, in their Long March, the Communists had sought escape from the pressure which Chiang Kai-shek's armies were exerting on them south of the Yangtze and established themselves in the Northwest. Chiang Kai-shek ordered Chang Hsüeh-liang to move against them, but the Communists persuaded some of the latter's troops that they should unite against the Japanese and so be able to return to Manchuria. When Chiang Kai-shek went north in December, 1936, to check on the progress of the anti-Communist campaign, Chang Hsüeh-liang took him captive. To obtain his release, Chiang Kai-shek agreed to call off the campaign against the Communists and to form with them a united front against the Japanese invaders.

Chinese popular agitation against Japanese aggression mounted. On the Japanese side, discontent was aggravated by the world-wide depression of the 1930's. The extremists among the Japanese seized control and decided to expel the Westerners from East Asia and to keep that vast region as a preserve for exploitation—ostensibly for the benefit of all the peoples in the area.

In July, 1937, the crisis was precipitated by a clash between Chinese and Japanese troops in the outskirts of Peiping. The full-scale Japanese invasion of China began. The Japanese were determined to eliminate Chiang Kai-shek and his supporters and to set up a regime which, like Manchukuo, would be subservient to them. They had the advantage of undisputed control of sea communications with their homeland, and superiority in air power, other munitions, industrial equipment to provide matériel, and a trained body of officers. By the end of 1937 they had taken Shanghai and Nanking; in the latter city the initial occupation was marked by wholesale rape and the slaughter of civilians and disarmed prisoners which shocked the world. Chiang Kai-shek and the remnants of his armies retreated first to Hankow and then to Chungking, a city on the Yangtze above the gorges of that river. In Chungking, protected by mountains from attack from the ground but still subject to air raids, he set up the capital of the Republic of China. In December of 1937 the Japanese, created in Nanking a régime headed by Wang Ching-wei, a former colleague of Sun Yat-sen, who had fallen out with Chiang Kai-shek; and staffed by Chinese who agreed to cooperate with them. Here, they insisted, was the only true Republic of China. In March, 1940, they celebrated, with much ceremony, the "return" of the "national government" to Nanking, and claimed that it represented the Kuomintang and was loyal to the program of Sun Yat-sen. That regime was easily persuaded to enter into a treaty with Japan in which each agreed to respect the other's territories and sovereignty and to cooperate in economic, cultural, and political measures and against Communism. The Nanking puppet also recognized Manchukuo and was recognized by the governments of Germany and Italy, then associated with Japan in World War II.

Japanese Pressure Mounts

The Japanese set about developing the resources of the portions of China which were under the puppet Nanking government. Through companies ostensibly under joint Chinese and Japanese ownership but which actually were Japanese, they took over shipping, railways, factories, and other economic enterprises. They reorganized the schools so that the Japanese language was taught and textbooks were revised to promote friendship with Japan. The Chinese were cavalierly handled and narcotics were extensively sold. But the Japanese administration was honeycombed with dissensions and corruption.

Parallel with their efforts to set up a regime they could control, the Japanese pressed their attack on Chiang Kai-shek and the government which he headed, and gradually they tightened the noose by which they were hoping to choke him. They established their mastery over most of the main ports and moved their lines farther inland. However, some supplies continued to reach Chiang Kai-shek by circuitous routes out of Hong Kong and the French possessions in Indo-China, and with much labor the "Burma Road" was constructed across difficult mountain terrain between that British possession and "free" China. But when, during the first year of World War II in Europe, the tides were running against the British and French armies, the Japanese succeeded in plugging the routes to "free" China from the outer world through the Burma Road and Indo-China. In April, 1941, when the U.S.S.R. was seeking to be freed from danger in the East, a nonaggression pact was concluded between Moscow and Tokyo. Japan, therefore, regarded herself relieved of her chronic fear of Russia. Late in 1941 and early in 1942 the Japanese believed themselves safe from any successful threat from the Occident.

Long committed to the "open door" in China, the United States was increasingly unfriendly to Japan's adventure in China. The American government progressively tightened its restrictions on permitting the Japanese to buy from its citizens supplies which could be used in its conquest of China. In December, 1941, Japan suddenly struck a crippling blow to the U.S. Navy in Pearl Harbor. Within a few days she had taken Hong Kong. By the middle of the summer of 1942 she had captured Singapore, the Netherlands East Indies, Burma, the Philippines, and Guam, and was threatening Australia. Her dream of a "Greater East Asia" and a "co-prosperity sphere" under her leadership appeared to be on the eve of realization.

However, the United States rallied its immense resources and through naval and air battles pushed the Japanese back from their outposts in the Pacific to their main islands, the Japanese navy was all but eliminated, and Tokyo was visited with saturation bombing. With British aid, supplies were transported to Chiang Kai-shek's armies across the "hump" of the mountains separating India from "free" China. The Ledo Road was constructed to bring in relief from India by the ground route. In August, 1945, Americans dropped atomic bombs on Hiroshima and Nagasaki, thus completing the defeat of Japan, which was followed by the occupation of her soil, theoretically by the Allied Powers but practically by the Americans. The evacuation of China by the Japanese was quickly accomplished thereafter.

During the years of mounting Japanese pressure the record in "free" China was mixed. On the one hand, great courage and ingenuity were shown in areas under the Republic of China. Refugees poured in from "occupied" China. Schools and universities transferred a large proportion of their staffs and students and part of their equipment to the West and there maintained vigorous if attenuated programs. For a time a thrill of adventure maintained morale. Improvements were registered in local governments, industrial cooperatives were organized, the growth of the opium poppy was curtailed, natural resources were surveyed, and the authority of the central government among the non-Chinese tribes and in Sinkiang was strengthened. In 1943 new treaties were negotiated by Chungking with the United States and Great Britain which canceled the extraterritoriality that had long been a source of friction. The United States repealed its exclusion acts against the Chinese, placed immigration on a quota basis, and permitted the naturalization of Chinese. Thanks to the United States, the Republic of China received the status of a great power. Chiang Kai-shek visited India and in 1943 participated at a consultation in Cairo with Prime Minister Churchill and President Roosevelt. When, after the war, the United Nations was created, one of the five permanent seats on the Security Council was assigned to the Republic of China.

On the other hand, in the prolonged strain of the war the Republic of China was badly weakened. Cut off from its previous revenues from the ports and business of East China, it was progressively impoverished, and inflation inevitably occurred. Factionalism, corruption, and inefficiency were rife. An increasing proportion of the support of the government was from the landlords of West China, and thereby the Republic of China laid itself open to the charge of alliance with the exploiters of the peasants. Although in theory the Kuomintang and the Communists were united in opposition to the Japanese, in reality Chungking's military resources were largely directed toward keeping guard against the Communists. In the meanwhile, the Communists were building a disciplined army inured by guerrilla resistance to the Japanese and were creating a unified party structure.

Officials of the Republic of China were humiliated by not being consulted at Yalta when the U.S.S.R., Great Britain, and the United States entered into an agreement for united action for the final crushing of Japan and in doing so consented to Russian terms which vitally affected China. By these terms Russia was to be accorded the holdings in Manchuria of which she had been deprived by her war of 1904-1905 with Japan and by later cessions to Japan. Dairen was to be internationalized with the recognition of the pre-eminent interests of Russia in that port, the lease on Port Arthur was to be returned to Russia, and the Manchurian railways were to be placed under joint Russo-Chinese management. The status quo in the Mongolian People's Republic (Outer Mongolia) was to be preserved. But Chinese sovereignty in Manchuria was recognized and the provisions concerning Outer Mongolia and Russian holdings in Manchuria were to require the concurrence of Chiang Kai-shek.

Appearances were partly preserved when, in August, 1945, after prolonged negotiations the Republic of China and the U.S.S.R. signed a treaty agreeing to collaborate in the common war against Japan, not to enter into any alliance directed against the other, to respect the sovereignty and territorial integrity of both countries, and not to interfere in the internal affairs of either. The treaty was to run for thirty years. In an exchange of notes China concurred in the disposition of Dairen, Port Arthur, and the Manchurian railways, which had been arranged at Yalta, and consented to the independence of Outer Mongolia if it was favored by a plebescite in that country.

The Failure to Achieve Reconstruction

In the summer of 1945 the Republic of China set about the difficult task of the reconstruction of the war-wasted country. In retrospect it is now clear that the effort was foredoomed. The Chiang Kai-shek regime was exhausted by the long years of resistance to Japan. Presumably only the help of the United States had saved it from complete collapse. Even in its heyday it had not had effective control over all China and now it endeavored to extend its administration over China proper, Manchuria, Taiwan, and Sinkiang. That ambitious goal required an experienced and honest administrative personnel which Chiang Kai-shek and those about him did not possess in sufficient quantity. In the regions that had been occupied by the Japanese, debilitating friction developed between the Chungking element, now put in charge, and the Chinese who had lived through the occupation and whom the former denounced or distrusted as collaborators with the recent enemy. Loud complaints were heard of the lack of democracy and the repression of dissident elements, especially students, by the Kuomintang. As we have seen, the governor put in charge of Taiwan was rapacious and corrupt, and executed prominent Taiwanese who seemed to be a threat to his rule. In Manchuria only the main cities could be held, for the Communists were infiltrating the countryside.

Through many agencies, governmental, philanthropic, and missionary, foreign friends of the Chinese sought to help. President Truman sent General George C. Marshall to seek a peaceful integration of the Kuomintang and the Communists in a stable government, but that honest and selfless attempt was defeated by the reciprocal hatreds and distrust of the two rivals, and civil war again erupted. In January, 1947, Marshall left China for Washington to become Secretary of State. In the summer of that year an American mission headed by General Albert C. Wedemeyer surveyed the situation. Wedemeyer spoke to Chiang Kai-shek and the Nationalists with a candor that had no regard for face, and made recommendations for an international administration of Manchuria which were plainly impossible to implement. The United States gave to the Kuomintang armies much help in military equipment, but the lack of morale among both troops and officers negated its usefulness.

The final blow to the Republic of China came from the failure to control inflation. An all-out effort for a sound currency was made with which many Chinese cooperated by the surrender of their gold, but which quickly failed. The Kuomintang had finally lost the confidence of the country; it had clearly sacrificed the mandate of Heaven. Now came the mastery of the mainland by the Communists.

For a comprehensive bibliography, covering all Chinese history and culture, including the Communist years, and predominantly of books and articles in English, see Charles O. Hucker, *China, a Critical Bibliography* (Tucson: The University of Arizona Press, 1962). Less extensive, but very useful, is Hucker's *Chinese History: A Bibliographical Review* (Washington: Service Center for Teachers of History, 1958). For a general survey, covering Chinese history from the beginning to 1963, with chapters on various aspects of Chinese culture, extensive bibliographies, and an index of Chinese characters, see Kenneth Scott Latourette, *The Chinese: Their History and Culture* (New York: The Macmillan Company, 4th edition, revised, 1964). An account of an early stage of the student and intellectual revolution is in Tse-tsung Chow, *The May Fourth Movement: Intellectual Revolution in Modern China* (Cambridge, Mass.: Harvard University Press, 1960). On the political history of China in the twentieth century through 1962, see O. Edmund Clubb, *Twentieth Century China* (New York, Columbia University Press, 1964).

The bibliography on China under the Communists is very extensive and of varied quality. A few items will give some indication of what is available: Robert S. Elegant, *China's Red Masters: Political Biographies of the Chinese Communist Leaders* (New York: Twayne Publishers, 1951) is useful. A book based on extensive research and intensely critical of communism is Richard L. Walker, *China under Communism: The First Five Years* (New Haven: Yale University Press, 1955). A more balanced view, growing out of extensive travel, by a French journalist, is

Tibor Mende, *China and Her Shadow* (New York: Coward-McCann, 1960), Edgar Snow's *The Other Side of the River* (New York: Random House, 1961) is a friendly, but not uncritical account, based on a visit to China in 1960. Very favorable, based on impressions from two trips, is Felix Greene, *The Wall Has Two Sides: A Portrait of China Today* (London: Jonathan Cape, 1962). See also, Yuan-li Wu, *Economic Development and the Use of Energy Resources in Communist China* (Hoover Institution, Stanford University, 1963); Peter Berton and Eugene Wu, *Contemporary China: A Research Guide* (Institute of Modern Asian Studies, University of Hong Kong, 1964), extremely valuable as a guide to the enormous mass of documentary material; Dan H. Jacobs and Hans H. Baerwald, editors, *Chinese Communism: Selected Documents* (New York, Harper & Row, 1963); and Cyril Birch, editor, *Chinese Communist Literature* (New York, Fredcrick A. Praeger, 1963).

A thoughtful survey, placing the People's Republic of China in its historical setting, and with an account of personal experiences by a Chinese who had much of his education in the United States and Great Britain, and who after a residence in the People's Republic of China left voluntarily and disillusioned, is Fu-sheng Wu, *The Wilting of the Hundred Flowers: The Chinese Intelligentsia under Mao* (New York: Frederick A. Praeger, 1962). Also useful are T. J. Hughes, *The Economic Development of Communist China, 1949-1958* (New York: Oxford University Press, 1959); A. Doak Barnett, *Communist China and Asia: Challenge to American Policy* (New York: Harper & Brothers, 1960); and Robert J. Lifton, *Thought Reform and the Psychology of Totalism: A Study of "Brainwashing" in China* (New York: W. W. Norton & Co., 1961).

Among the many books on Sino-Soviet Relations, see Donald S. Zagoria, *The Sino-Soviet Conflict, 1956-1961* (Princeton, N. J.: Princeton University Press, 1962), and G. F. Hudson, Richard Lowenthal, and Roderick MacFarquhar, *The Sino-Soviet Dispute* (New York: Fredcrick A. Praeger, 1961).

For a period of American relations, see Kenneth Scott Latourette, *The American Record in the Far East, 1945-1951* (New York: The Macmillan Company, 1952), and for a more detailed account of China in the same period, see Herbert Feis, *The China Tangle: The American Effort in China from Pearl Harbor to the Marshall Mission* (Princeton, N. J.: Princeton University Press, 1953). A more comprehensive survey of relations with the United States is in John K. Fairbank, *The United States and China* (Cambridge, Mass.: Harvard University Press, revised edition, 1958).

For translations of pertinent documents, see Mao Tse-tung, *Selected Works* (4 vols., New York; International Publishers, 1954-56); Conrad Brandt, Benjamin Schwartz, and John K. Fairbank, A *Documentary History of Chinese Communism* (Cambridge, Mass.: Harvard University Press, 1952); and E. Stuart Kirby, *Contemporary China: Economic and Social Studies: Documents, Bibliography, Chronology* (Hong Kong: 3 vols., 1955-59).

Among the many periodicals are *The China Quarterly* (London, The Summit House, 1960), mostly on the contemporary scene and inclined to be critical of communism; and *The Journal of Asian Studies* (Ann Arbor, Mich., 1956-   ), the organ of the association for Asian studies, succeeding *The Far Eastern Quarterly*, published by The Far Eastern Association, covering the entire range of East Asian history and culture, and especially valuable for excellent book reviews.

In addition to the survey in Latourette, *The Chinese: Their History and Culture*, the following are among the hundreds of books which deal with specific aspects of geography, pre-nineteenth century culture, and events in the first half of the twentieth century: George B. Cressey, *Land of the 500 Million: A Geography of China* (New York: McGraw-Hill Book Co., 1955); William Theodore de Bary, Wing-tsit Chan, and Burton Watson, compilers, *Sources of Chinese Tradition* (New York: Columbia University Press, 1960), a superb collection of translations of excerpts of Chinese thought and literature across the centuries; Arthur F. Wright, *Buddhism in Chinese History* (Stanford: Stanford University Press, 1959); and Wright, editor, *The Confucian Persuasion* (Stanford: Stanford University Press, 1960); Mary C. Wright, *The Last Stand of Chinese Conservatism: The T'ung-Chih Restoration, 1862-1874* (Stanford, Calif.; Stanford University Press, 1957); Kenneth Scott Latourette, A *History of Christian Missions in China* (New York: The Macmillan Co.); John Hersey, A *Single Pebble* (New York: Alfred A. Knopf, 1956), a fictionalized description of traditional Chinese attitudes; Victor Purcell, *The Boxer Uprising: A Background Study* (Cambridge University Press, 1963); Sun Yat-sen, *San Min Chu I: The Three Principles of the People*, trans. F. W. Price, ed. by L. T. Chen (Shanghai: China Committee, Institute of Pacific Relations, 1927); Lyon Sharman, *Sun Yat-sen, His Life and Its Meaning: A Critical Biography* (New York: The John Day Co., 1934); and Wesley R. Fishel, *The End of Extraterritoriality in China* (Berkeley: University of California Press, 1952).

INDEX

Abacus, the, 70
Age, respect for, 85-86
Agriculture, 9-11, 42, 93-95
Alexander the Great, 101
All-China Athletic Association, 19
All-China Federation of Democratic Women, 19
All-China Federation of Literary and Art Circles, 19
All-China Federation of Trade Unions, 19
Anfu Club, 128
Annam, efforts to control, 26-27
Antibiotics, 11
Aquinas, Saint Thomas, 69
Atomic weapons, 32, 33

Bandung Conference, the, 29, 33
Banking, 95-96
Belgium, treaty with China, 108
Birth control, 12
Boxer Protocol, 121-22
Buddhism: affects of, on Chinese culture, 62-63; and the Chinese Communist Party, 7-8, 22-23; and Neo-Confucianism, 69; and the New Tide, 133; in South Vietnam, 27-28; under Ch'ing dynasty, 91-92; under Han, 61; under T'ang, 65

Buddhist Association, 7
Burma Road, 140

Calligraphy, 98
Castro, Fidel, 37
Central Committee, 18-19
Ceramics, 98-99
Chang Hsüeh-liang, 4, 135-36, 138
Chang Hsün, 127-28
Chang Tso-lin, 135
Ch'ang-an (city), 64-65
Chefoo Convention, 115-16
Ch'ên Tu-hsiu, 2
Ch'en Yi, 3, 30
Chiang Kai-shek, 1, 2, 3, 30, 40-43, 139-43
Ch'ien Lung Emperor, 79-80
Child marriage, 17
Ch'in dynasty, 57-58
Chin dynasty, 67
China: earliest culture of, 50-51; geography of, 45-47; and the Mongols, 67-68, 71-73; natural resources, 45-47; origin of word, 57; outlying dependencies, 47-49; recurring features in thought of, 53-54; shaping of culture, 53-57; treaties, 106-12; unification, 57-62; war with France, 108-10; war with Great Britain, 104-10;

San Min Chu I (Sun Yat-sen), 42, 134
Science, 99
Secret societies, 86
Sepoy Mutiny, 109
Shang Ti, 51
Shansi bankers, 95
Shih Huang Ti, 57-58
Silk, 98, 104
Silver, 104-105
Sinkiang, 22, 29, 47-49
Sino-Soviet Friendship General Association, 31
Soong, T. V., 135
South East Asia Treaty Organization, 34
Southeast Asia, 26-30
Sports, 88
Ssŭ-ma Ch'ien, 60
Stalin, Joseph, 4, 30, 31, 32
Sui dynasty, 63-64
Sun Yat-sen, 1, 3, 42; background, 125; death, 134; elected president, 125, 128; flees to Japan, 127; resigns, 126; San Min Chu I, 42, 134
Sung dynasty, 66-70; conquered by Mongols, 67; cultural achievements, 69-70; economic prosperity, 67; philosophy, 69-70; war with the Chin, 67
Supreme People's Court, 19, 20
Supreme People's Procuratorate, 19, 20

Ta Ch'ing, 20
T'ai P'ing Rebellion, 113, 114
T'ai Shan, 91
Taiwan, 34, 35, 40-43; economic development, 43; language, 41, 42; population, 42
T'ang dynasty, 49, 64-66
Tao, the, 56
Tao Tê Ching, the, 56
Taoism, 7-8, 56, 69, 91-92
Tea, 104
Temuchin, 67
Theater, 71-72, 88
Thirty-eighth parallel, the, 25-26

Tibet, 22-24, 29, 47-49
Tito, Marshal, 37
Tobacco, 102
Trade: in China proper, 48; foreign, 103-105, 108-109, 115; reorganization of, 12-14; under Ch'ing dynasty, 95; under Han, 60; under Ming dynasty, 73-75
Truman, Harry, 26, 40, 143
Tsêng Kuo-fan, 114
Tso Tsung-t'ang, 114
Tsungli-yamen, the, 115
Tuan Ch'i-jui, 127-28
T'ung Chih Emperor, 114
Twenty-one Demands, 129, 130
Tz'ŭ Hsi, 114, 118, 120-21, 123-24

Ungern, Baron, 21
Union of Soviet Socialist Republics: aid to Communist China, 14; and Chinese students, 15; conflict with People's Republic of China, 26, 30-35; influence, 18; and Japan, 35-36; and Korea, 25-26; and Mongolia, 21-22; and Tibet, 22, 23; treaty with China, 109-10; war with Japan, 122
United Nations: and the independence of Mongolia, 128; and Korea, 25-26, 34, 38; and People's Republic of China, 37-38; and Republic of China, 41; and Tibet, 23
United States of America: "the open door policy," 120; and People's Republic of China, 6, 25-26, 31, 34-36, 37; and Republic of China, 4, 35; and South Vietnam, 27; and Taiwan, 43; treaties with China, 107, 109-10; war with Japan, 140

Vatican, the, 7
Vietminh, 27

Wang An-shih, 68-69
Wang Ching-wei, 139
Water mills, 63
Wedemeyer, Albert C., 143